VICTORY
I N
SPIRITUAL WARFARE

GARY WHETSTONE

VICTORY IN SPIRITUAL WARFARE

How Jesus Sets You Free

Creation House
Lake Mary, Florida

Creation House
Strang Communications Company
600 Rinehart Road
Lake Mary, FL 32746
(407) 333-0600

All Scripture quotations are from the Holy Bible, New International Version, unless otherwise noted. Copyright © 1973, 1978, 1984, International Bible Society. Used by permission. Scripture quotations marked KJV are from the King James Version of the Bible.

First Printing, February 1990
Second Printing, May 1990

Contents

1/   Madman on the Loose..................................7

2/   All-American Boy......................................11

3/   Born Again...17

4/   On the Run...21

5/   Solid Ground..27

6/   The Power of God.....................................33

7/   Works of Darkness....................................39

8/   The How and Why of Demonic Activity........43

9/   Demonic Deception...................................49

10/   The Truth About Satan..............................55

11/   Power and Authority................................61

12/   New Creation Life...................................65

13/   Unmasking the Enemy..............................69

14/   Binding and Loosing................................75

15/   In the Name of Jesus................................81

16/   Victory Over the Sin Nature......................85

17/   The Life of Triumph.................................93

Handbook for Spiritual Warfare....................101

1

Madman on the Loose

Wham! Wham! Bang!

"What's that?" The pounding from the front porch startled Tom Craig.

"Somebody's trying to break open the door!" Tom's wife, Linda, shrieked in panic.

The wood molding gave way in a shower of splinters as a booted foot crashed against it, and the door swung open. Silhouetted against the yellow glare of the streetlight stood the hulking figure of a man.

"I own this house! It's mine!" roared the intruder. His eyes flashed as they roamed from one side of the room to the other, pausing briefly to glare at Tom.

"What? Who are you?" Tom almost choked in dread at the sight of the frightful apparition. As his eyes focused on the figure, Tom noticed the wild, intense blue eyes, then the tangled reddish-brown hair and the bushy beard. He looked like a barbarian, a pirate! But this pirate wore the ragged T-shirt, torn jeans and matching denim vest typical of the motorcycle gangs that roamed the Wilmington, Delaware, neighborhood.

"Shut up!" the bearded thug demanded, as he strode across the threshold. He was no more than twenty years old, but he stood six inches taller than Tom. "I said this is my house!" the madman repeated, swinging his arm in an arc. He pointed to the furniture, a piece at a time. "That's my couch! That's my chair! That's my table! That's my lamp!"

Tom couldn't believe what was happening: Who is this monster? Why has he invaded my house? He must be insane—perhaps strung out on dope—obviously dangerous. He's bigger than I am. Can I stop him—get him out of here—without being killed?

Horrible fear gripped Linda. Her petite body began to shake, ninety-eight pounds of trembling terror. Beads of sweat popped out on her forehead. She was dumbstruck, paralyzed with fear.

The intruder turned to look at Linda, leering with lust. "And that's my wife, and I'm gonna' have her!" He lurched toward the terrified woman.

Tom sprang forward. "No, you don't!"

The intruder's foot flashed upward, catching the shocked husband in the stomach. Tom dropped to his knees and rolled in a ball on the floor, gasping in pain.

The intruder seemed powerful beyond his size. He grabbed Linda and flung her onto the couch, then pounced on her, covering her screaming mouth with his grimy hand. His intent was clear.

Fear and rage produced a rush of adrenaline that spurred Tom into action. He struggled to his feet, hobbled to the hall closet, jerked open the door and grabbed his shotgun. Then Tom turned toward the intruder and yelled, "Leave her alone, or I'll kill you!"

The madman roared, leaped to his feet and rushed at Tom, ignoring the shotgun. The two grappled, cursing, slugging, kicking. Tom finally succeeded in clubbing the intruder with the shotgun, momentarily stunning him.

"For God's sake, call the police, Linda!" Tom ordered. She jumped up from the couch and stumbled down the hallway.

The bearded man roared in pain, shook his head and sprang to his feet to attack the householder once more. Tom dodged his onrushing charge. The attacker tripped over an ottoman and crashed into the fish tank, splattering its ten gallons of watery contents all over the wall and carpet.

Tom hurled himself onto the water-soaked man. They squirmed and cursed and struggled together. Tom finally pinned the assailant's arms to his sides.

"Had enough?" Tom asked.

"Yeah, yeah," grunted his opponent.

Tom eased his grip. With a surge of strength the intruder wrenched free and ran out the door into the chilly September night. Tom grabbed the shotgun and raced after him.

"Oh, no, you don't! You're not getting away!" shouted Tom. He swung the gun over his head as he closed in on the fleeing man.

Thud. The gun butt made contact; the intruder was down for the count.

When the fallen man opened his eyes, he was staring up the length of the shotgun, the muzzle jammed inside his mouth. "Don't move a muscle, sucker, or I'll blow your brains out!'' he heard Tom growl. Then the man, his face filled with rage, snarled, ''Go ahead and kill me!'' Pinned against the fence, he tried in desperation to force Tom to pull the trigger and end this tormented existence. He kicked Tom in the groin, but Tom somehow maintained his pose and did not pull the trigger.

Within minutes four heavily armed policemen—a special SWAT team—arrived at the scene, had the madman in hand-cuffs and dragged him to one of their cruisers.

I was that madman.

The names of Tom and Linda Craig are fictitious. But the events of that night in September 1971 really took place. Due to my deranged condition, some of the details remain fuzzy, though I can still remember the taste of that shotgun barrel.

Incredible as it may seem, I am completely normal now—sane, rational, reasonable. In fact, I am the pastor of a fast-growing church in my hometown of New Castle, Delaware. Imagine that! Pastoring in the same area in which these events took place!

What brought about my insane, violent behavior in the first place? It's a story that will help you understand the severity of the drug problem and the wildness on the streets of our cities. And what brought about my recovery? It's a story that will amaze you, a story of the Lord's grace that will bring glory to our miracle-working God.

2

All-American Boy

In 1968 I was basically the all-American boy. My high school grades were good. I served as president of the student council. A wiry 120-pounder, I excelled in sports. I was captain of the freshman football team. I held several backstroke records for the swim team. I was number two in the state tennis championship. Everything was rosy, and my future looked bright—until one fateful day.

Sledding is a wonderful winter activity. My friends and I enjoyed racing down the slopes. I didn't intend to slide out of control into the path of a car, but it happened. I slammed head-on into an automobile, my right arm driven through my back.

The doctors at the hospital did everything they could to repair the damage. They removed a chest muscle and sewed it around my back. They saved my arm. But its movement was limited. That meant the end of my swimming and football careers. It also meant the end of tennis competition: I could still play, but I had lost my overpowering serve.

Academics was the only area in which I still did well. Unfortunately, that didn't mean much to my peers. My friends at Conrad High School were looking for the athletic type. I had difficulty relating to their social circle and, as a result, I became insecure. I lost interest in my position as president of the student council. My grades slipped from A's and B's to C's and D's.

During the time I was in the tenth grade my whole self-perception was ruined. I grew to be five feet, ten inches tall but I saw myself as half a person.

My brother, Wick, was six years older than I was. By this time he was twenty-two and president of the Pagans' motorcycle club, with several hundred members ranging from Wilmington to South Philadelphia. He became my idol, and the Pagans were my best friends and "protectors."

Most of the Pagans rode Harley-Davidson "hogs," but I rode a lighter-weight motorcycle. The Harleys were too heavy for me to handle comfortably. But no other part of the Pagans' life-style was too heavy for me. The drugs, the sex orgies, the gun dealing—I bought it all. To my twisted way of thinking, conforming to their way of living would gain me respect within the group. I did not hesitate to live the life of an outlaw.

Money was easy. Guns, drugs and sex always provided the life-style we demanded. If you wanted it, we had it or could get it—from assault guns to kilos of the most powerful South American drugs available. Our trade thrived, and the price was always right. And there was danger. I always carried a .38 caliber pistol and, frequently, a Derringer, depending upon whom I would be seeing.

During my weapons training, I became proficient in the use of certain automatic weapons and explosives.

Since I had easy access to drugs, I was always "high." It wasn't long before I was using up to five hits of acid a day. Little by little, my mind deteriorated.

Gradually I became filled with aggression, fear and hatred. By the time I reached the eleventh grade many of my friends—gang members—were in prison or had been murdered. I was paranoid. I had trouble relating in normal society. At times I went into uncontrollable rages. I frequently became confused and could no longer distinguish right from wrong. I experienced terrifying hallucinations, heard weird voices and carried out the voices' mandates.

My parents were at a loss as to know what to do. They committed me to the Delaware State Hospital for psychiatric treatment and drug rehabilitation. As soon as I was released, I resumed my pattern of drug abuse, and they committed me again, and then again. I was admitted to and released from the mental hospital four times before I finished the eleventh grade.

Somehow I managed to graduate from high school in 1971, but my behavior became thoroughly antisocial. My obsession caused me to believe I possessed things that did not belong to me. For example, one night, while driving my van through a local neighborhood, I saw a pickup truck with two nice outside mirrors on it. I stopped my van, got my tool chest out and started removing the mirrors from the pickup truck.

A passerby asked me, "What are you doing?"

"These are *my* mirrors!" I screamed, cursing. "They fit *my* truck!" I finished removing them and calmly drove away.

This off-the-wall behavior persisted for several months. It culminated when I kicked in the door of "Tom and Linda Craig's" home about six blocks from my parents' house, terrifying the occupants with claims that I owned the house, its contents, and even the wife.

This escapade resulted in my being made a ward of the state. I was so deranged that I spent most of my hospital time in isolation in a padded cell.

Life in a padded cell is horrible beyond imagining. An insane person often will tear off his clothes, bang his head against the walls and otherwise attempt to injure himself. He will sometimes smear his feces all over the cell. Meals are shoved to the patient through a slot in the door, and the inmate will use the plate for a toilet. The guards have to restrain the patient physically whenever they hose out the filth from the cell. That was how I existed.

During this time my mental condition was analyzed by the psychiatrists. In their final evaluation they declared me hopelessly insane. Following this evaluation, the state committed me to the mental institution for the rest of my life.

The hospital authorities contacted my parents and confronted them with the findings. Since my condition was considered hopeless, the doctors proposed putting me into an extreme experimental program. I would be subjected to intense electrotherapy, receiving powerful shocks directed toward certain control centers of my brain. My violent behavior would disappear, and I would become manageable.

But the consequences would be severe. My mind would be reduced to that of a three-year-old child, and I would never again have control over my speech or actions. Basically, the doctors were asking my parents for permission to reduce their son to a guinea pig for scientific research.

Perhaps because I had put them through such hell, and because they were told there was no hope I would ever recover, my parents agreed to the experiment. They signed the waiver stating that if the state of Delaware killed or permanently maimed me they would hold no legal recourse against the state.

The top psychiatrist brought me into a meeting with my parents, with the goal of explaining to me the experiment for which I was now to be scheduled. Most days I was bound in fetters—heavily woven fabric restraints that held my arms and legs as firmly as handcuffs and leg irons, but without inflicting the cuts and bruises that metal manacles cause. But on that particular day I was free from restraints. As the doctor began his explanation, I was swept up in another uncontrollable rage. I hurled myself at the doctor, attempting to destroy him. The guards sprang upon me in an instant and subdued me. I soon found myself back in isolation.

That was on a Wednesday, and it was the end of any attempt at explanation. In two days the procedure would begin. It would take several weeks in all, because the doctors did not want to give me the entire treatment at once. They said a slower process would enable me to maintain my motor coordination. I would still be able to walk, even though I would not retain my memory or ability to speak. Ultimately, that would be my future.

Or would it? Jesus says, "The Son gives life to whom he is pleased to give it" (John 5:21). I was about to be given life.

3

Born Again

When I was committed to the state mental hospital, it made the news. To most who saw the account, the report held little significance—another nut hauled off to the asylum. But to some of my former high school classmates, the news seemed tragic. True, I had befriended none of them. True, I was surly and strange to most of them. But I was a classmate, and we had a thread or two in common.

A number of these kids attended the same Baptist church. Several of them discussed what had befallen me. What could they do? Pray? Yes, they did that. After a midweek service some of these youthful Christians urged their pastor, Ron

Hayden, to visit me. After all, ministers were allowed to visit patients in the state mental hospital even if ordinary young people weren't.

So it was that the next day, Thursday, Ron Hayden was waiting in the solarium to see me. Why had it been so simple to arrange? Perhaps the authorities decided that one last contact with a religious leader was the least they could do for a person about to be reduced to a vegetable. Sort of like "last rites."

I was removed from isolation and taken to meet the preacher. I must have been a shocking, pathetic sight to behold. I shuffled along on unsteady legs, my shoulder-length red hair and my tangled beard sticking out through my inmate's garb. To quiet me, I had been heavily sedated. Spittle drooled from the corner of my mouth. In this kind of stupor I was not a threat to anyone, so I was free from physical restraints during this visitation.

When I made my shuffling entrance, the pastor sat down. Then, looking directly at me, he said words that seemed to cut through the fog that clouded my mind. "Gary," he said, "I know exactly what's wrong with you."

He caught me by surprise. Never had anyone said that to me before. Every psychiatrist, every psychologist, every psychoanalyst whom I had seen had been unable to figure out what was really wrong with me. Instead they placed labels on me—paranoid, psychotic, and so forth. Now labeling a disorder may bring some satisfaction to a doctor. But it doesn't offer much hope to the patient. Now, suddenly, this preacher was claiming that he could identify what was wrong with me.

"It's the power of sin," Hayden said simply. "The power of sin is going to kill you."

Drugged though I was, his words pierced through to me. I listened to what he was saying.

"If you believe in your heart that Jesus Christ died for you, and that He rose from the dead," the preacher continued, "and if you confess with your mouth that Jesus is Lord, you'll have a new life."

That's all I heard. But it was all I needed to hear. I have no way of knowing how that preacher saw me that day, whether he saw me as a hopeless case or as a genuine prospect for salvation. I have no way of knowing whether he was just presenting a gospel invitation in a mechanical way, or whether he experienced a profound sense of anointing. All I know is that he said what I needed to hear. Somehow the Lord gave power to those words so that they penetrated my deepest self.

I fell to my knees on the floor, sobbing. I called on Jesus to come into my heart. Yes, I believed He died for me. Yes, I believed He rose from the dead. Yes, I did confess with my mouth that Jesus is Lord.

After a few minutes I regained control of myself. I stood up. Everything was different. I knew that, despite being overloaded with drugs, my mind was sound.

I looked at the preacher through tear-filled eyes. "Do you know what happened to me?" I asked.

"Yes," he said. "You were born again." He made no attempt to explain what that meant.

"Well, our time is up," he added. "May God bless you." And just like that he was gone.

4

On the Run

After Ron Hayden's visit, I was wrapped in restraints once again. But now I had a different problem from the one I'd had before. Now I was a normal person imprisoned in a mental hospital.

I tried to convince people that I was sane but no one would listen. When I returned to my cell, I beat on the walls to get someone's attention, but I was ignored. Since I had beaten on the walls many times before, they probably thought this time wasn't any different.

The next day I was taken to see the head psychiatrist. I tried to explain the spiritual experience I'd had. But the doctor said, "Gary, I'm sorry. With the tremendous level of instability you're displaying, it is very common for someone to imagine a religious encounter. This is just another manifestation of all the problems you're experiencing. It doesn't matter if it's religion you're getting involved in or something else. All of those things are a crutch for someone like you. Until you learn how to behave in society, none of those things will work. We're still going through with the process."

At that point I became so frustrated with the doctor that I attacked him. Now that kind of behavior may seem shocking. I was supposed to have been born again, and born-again people don't act violently, do they? Well, I did. I was born again, but I didn't know any other way to release my anxiety. My spiritual training was zero.

Following my assault, the doctor wrote in his book, "No change." That was the end of our meeting.

As I was being led back to the isolation area, something inside me said, "Run! Run!" I thought, Run? Where am I going to go? It's snowing outside, and I'm in my bare feet. I have on a state hospital shirt with hospital pants—and the doors are locked.

I stopped walking and looked around. Again I asked myself, Where am I going to run? Suddenly my attention was drawn to a nearby door. It had been unbolted, and the chains had been taken off! Once more I heard the word, "Run!" At that moment I felt a surge of energy and I took off running.

There was no natural explanation for what happened next. The guards who were posted to watch me did not try to stop me, even though they were physically standing there watching as I escaped. Did God blind their eyes?

I darted through the door and headed toward the commissary, where the more trusted patients were standing around. I ran through yelling, "I'm on the run! I'm on the run!"

Then the patients lifted up their voices and pounded their fists on the tables, shouting in unison: "Run! Run! Run! Run!" The sound echoed in the commissary hall as two of the braver patients ran with me.

"Take my coat!" one yelled.

"Here're my shoes!" the other one shouted.

As they tossed them to me, I stopped and quickly put on the big old boat shoes and the heavy army pea coat.

I continued running. Not too far in the distance I could see a guard shack. I realized that anyone with long red hair and a beard, state hospital pants, shoes that didn't fit and an oversized coat definitely looked like an escapee. Even though I was afraid, I slowed down and walked past the guard house as though nothing were wrong. I walked as if I belonged outside those gates.

And I did belong out there. When that Baptist pastor left, I didn't know what had happened to me. I had become God's child. The moment I became born again, all of God's promises began working in my life. God promises to deliver us from the kingdom of darkness into the kingdom of light. God literally delivered me from the mental hospital by unlocking that door!

After I passed the guard house and reached Route 40, I ran as fast as I could. But I soon realized I wasn't going to get very far on foot before the police caught up with me. So I decided to find a ride.

Straight ahead I saw a man in his pickup truck waiting at a stoplight. He seemed to be the most likely candidate to take me home, so I ran to the truck, opened the passenger door, jumped inside and said, "Take me home."

The man looked at me. "You look like you're in trouble," he said.

I said, "No, not me. Everything's all right. I'm doing great!" Of course he knew that I was from the asylum. How could I hide with the clothes that I was wearing and a label that said, "State Hospital"?

But instead of putting me out, the man gave me a ride home. I had him drop me off a few blocks away, because I expected him to call the police.

How do you explain a complete stranger's willingness to transport a man who is obviously an escapee from a mental hospital? It doesn't make sense—unless you add God to the equation. He can make people act in a manner contrary to their normal course of behavior.

When I reached my parents' house, no one was home. I broke in, got some clothes and money, and took the keys to my old van.

I drove the van to Florida.

Again I realize that a church-going, law-abiding reader is going to be perplexed by my conduct. Here I am, a born-again follower of Jesus. I had escaped from the mental hospital, coerced a stranger into giving me a ride, and was involved in breaking and entering (even though it was my parents' home). I can only say that in my spiritual infancy these actions seemed perfectly logical to me. Certainly law-breaking cannot be condoned as acceptable behavior for new converts. I am simply reporting what I did.

While I was in Florida, my brother found out that some of my previous associates were planning to kill me. They thought I would turn state's evidence against them if I ever got caught by the police. These were the people I thought I could trust, and now they wanted me out of the way. There was also an all-points-bulletin out on me, so I couldn't go anyplace without being in danger.

My brother contacted a lawyer in the state of Delaware who did everything possible to have the state overturn its judgment against me, but the lawyer did not succeed.

I'm tired of running, I thought. Since I had been with

fugitives before, I knew what it was like to run. How am I ever going to get out of this thing? I wondered.

Even though I didn't know how, I finally decided to pray. I said, "Lord Jesus, if this experience with You is real, then I want to return to Delaware."

And I did.

When I arrived in my hometown, I was stopped by a policeman who had known me since childhood. "Gary!" the officer said as he looked into the van.

I gazed back at him and said, "Hi." He wasn't exactly the person I wanted to meet at three o'clock in the morning. I told the officer, "Look, whatever you do, don't arrest me. I'm going to park my van and sleep in it for the night. In the morning my parents are taking me back to the mental hospital." Wonder of wonders—he didn't turn me in!

The next morning I went back to the state hospital. When I arrived there, the officials looked at me strangely. Their expressions seemed to say, I can't believe this guy is back!

I told them there were several things I wanted. "Please don't give me any drugs," I said. "Put me in a mixed, open ward and give me every psychological test available. I intend to prove to you that I am sane!"

The Bible says that God has not given us a spirit of fear, but of power, love and a sound mind (see 2 Tim. 1:7). At that time I didn't know this verse. But I knew my mind was sound. Since I had come back of my own free will, the psychiatrists decided they didn't have anything to lose. Therefore, they fulfilled my requests.

When all of the tests were completed, the psychiatrists said they couldn't find anything wrong! They even showed me a comparison of previous tests to those which I had just taken. It was as if the results belonged to two different people.

Because my body was releasing chemicals that were different from before, the doctors concluded something was still wrong. I believe the Holy Ghost was just straightening out my body chemistry—giving me an overdose in one area to balance my system in another.

Nevertheless, because of the confusion about my results, the doctors decided that I must have a brain tumor. To solve this problem, I was given two choices. The first option was to let them cut the top of my head off and do a craniotomy, an exploratory surgery to find the tumor. The other choice was to have a pneumoencephalogram, a special X-ray of my head. Since I didn't like the idea of walking around bald, I decided to have the pneumo done.

After completing the X-ray, the doctors still could not find anything wrong. They even told me, "We can't figure out what's wrong with you, because there's nothing wrong with you!"

I was released from the hospital. But I still didn't fit in on the outside.

5

Solid Ground

My spiritual problem was quite basic: I had received Jesus as my Savior, but I had not bowed to Him as my Lord. When I prayed that fateful day at the mental hospital, Jesus cleansed my sinful past and made me a new creation, a son of God. But I had yet to find and fulfill my new identity.

Most people have a basic understanding of what a Christian acts like. I, however, did not know. We all know that many church-attenders act like Christians without having been born again. With me it was just the opposite. I was born again but I wasn't acting like a Christian.

Many people are content if their conduct merely appears to be Christian. They don't smoke or drink (at least not excessively), they don't do dope, and they don't engage in sexual misbehavior. On the positive side, they attend church, perhaps sing in the choir, and associate with those on the same rung of the social ladder. Other credits could be added to this list. But all fall short of bowing to the total lordship of Jesus.

In psychology the word *persona* means the outer personality or facade presented to others by an individual. In spiritual matters, Jesus seeks to change the person, not just the persona. He is more concerned with my *being* a son of God than with my acting like a Christian while being a child of the devil. In short, Jesus wants to reign in my heart as king of all that I am and all that I do. And He wants the same of you.

So how does Jesus obtain the throne in our hearts?

First, one must understand which part of us actually becomes born again. Jesus said, "That which is born of the flesh is flesh; and that which is born of the Spirit is spirit" (John 3:6, KJV).

Obviously, when a child is born, he takes on the image and likeness of his earthly parents; thus the flesh is born, but the remainder of the verse says that the Spirit bears a spirit. What this means is that your human spirit is born by God's Holy Spirit and now can receive all His benefits as a child of God. Satan is no longer your spiritual father since you have received Jesus but, as personal Savior and Lord, *God is*.

In John 1:12-13 we read, "Yet to all who received him, to those who believed in his name, he gave the right to become children of God—children born not of natural descent, nor of human decision or a husband's will, but born of God." This clearly shows God as our spiritual father.

We now have a new conflict because our human spirits have become born again, but our minds have not yet changed. This is why we need to understand that we are three-part beings. The spirit is the recreated part born from the Holy Spirit. The soul is comprised of the mind, will and emotions. Our bodies are the physical house we live in.

Our minds submit to God in a way different from that of our spirits. The mind must be renewed by hearing and understanding the Word of God before a real transformation takes place.

The apostle Paul writes, "Do not conform any longer to the pattern of this world, but be transformed by the renewing of your mind. Then you will be able to test and approve what God's will is—his good, pleasing and perfect will" (Rom. 12:2). The renewal process is like stripping the many layers of paint from an old chair. After the facade of paint is removed, the true beauty of the wood is revealed.

The soul comes to Jesus with layers of ignorance, pride, self-centeredness and a fixed determination to go its own way. After the confrontation with His Word, the once-hard layers melt away, and the soul comes to Jesus in free and hearty submission, desiring only to come under the government of King Jesus for all time to come.

I had yet to experience that kind of transformation. I was a son of God but I was still walking after my own fleshly desires, unaware of what God expected His sons to be.

I had been baptized in water, but it was as if I didn't "fit in" to Christianity, because I couldn't tell anyone all that I had gone through. I wasn't the most reputable person around, and there wasn't anyone who would listen to me. I certainly couldn't go back to my old friends. They thought I was crazy anyway: "What's all this religious stuff that Gary's talking about?" I felt stranded. My spiritual life was at a standstill, if not moving backwards.

All this time I was dating my future wife. In May 1972 Faye and I were married.

Then the bottom dropped out again. Just as one match can burn down an entire building, so can one careless mistake change one's direction in life. I smoked only one joint of marijuana at a small party, and the result was total chaos. I was harassed by the same confusing spirits that had attacked me in the past. By October 1975, Faye and I were separated, and we later divorced because of these problems. I didn't know what to do.

In the meantime God had been at work in my mother's life. She had been attending a Wednesday afternoon Bible study sponsored by a group of Catholic charismatic people. She was born again, and then she was baptized in the Holy Spirit.

One day my mother told me, "Gary, you've got demons in you." I thought, Gee, Mom, thanks for the good news. She continued, "You've got a choice. You can go back to the state hospital or you can get those demons cast out of you." Since I had already been to the state hospital and knew what the plans were there, I opted for the second choice.

I decided to attend a church service at a nearby independent charismatic church. At that meeting I was baptized in the Holy Spirit and I started speaking in other tongues. I didn't know what was happening. I just knew it was terrific!

But my troubles were far from over.

I had already attempted suicide twice. I want you to know that even born-again people can commit suicide. Satan will deceive and confuse anyone if he can. I was a believer! I may not have been a very strong believer, but I still believed. I still had Jesus in my heart. And now I was baptized in the Holy Spirit. But I was experiencing bouts of terrible depression.

I recall vividly my third attempt at suicide. It was in the

fall of 1975. In the midst of a deep depression I drove my Volkswagen onto a railway crossing and stopped, waiting for the train to come and slam me into eternity. I told God that only He could save me from death. I knew that it was Satan who was trying to kill me again, but without the knowledge required to stop him, I was again yielding to his plans of destruction. Then I heard a voice deep within me say, "You shall not die, but live, and declare the works of the Lord."

Soon I heard the rumble of the approaching train. I shut my eyes in anticipation of the crash. But nothing happened. The huge engine rushed past my car on a second set of tracks, a few feet from where I was parked. I learned later that the train had been temporarily rerouted to the other tracks during some repair work.

Thoroughly shaken I drove to my ex-wife's mobile home. I told her what had happened and begged her to take me to a private mental clinic to prevent another suicide attempt. I was desperate.

Near the end of my two-week stay in the clinic, a local charismatic pastor, knowledgeable in the ministry of deliverance, came to see me at my request. This pastor, who also had a degree in clinical psychology, recognized that my battle was not psychological, but due to demonic activity. He arranged for a Spirit-filled layman to join with him in casting out the demons that had been driving me to self-destruction.

Following this time of ministry, I stayed in the clinic two days. When I left, I was totally delivered from the tormenting spirits. It was then that I realized something important. My mother was right. Satan was the originator of the problems I had experienced for so many years. He was the source.

Now that I was delivered, I began to fast, pray and claim God's Word for my marriage to be restored. God honored my faith in His Word: Faye was born again and filled with the Holy Spirit. In July 1976 we were remarried.

For the next four years, my attention was focused on gaining new insights into the Word of God and in devoting quality time to my wife, whom I now treasured, and our two beloved children, Eric and Laurie.

During this period of time, tragedy struck. My mother died after a long illness, and six months later my father had a heart attack and died suddenly.

Overnight Faye and I became guardians of my fifteen-year-old brother, Chris. Thank God for the knowledge of His Word that produces stability in our lives. No longer would the winds of adversity blow me off my foundation in Christ.

I left my job as a welder and went into business. God's blessing was evident. The business thrived. For the first time, I felt that I was standing on solid ground during three years of prosperity and great responsibility in the business community.

Our lives were, indeed, built upon a good foundation—Christ, the solid rock. God led me to begin several businesses which prospered, and still we remained firm and stable upon our foundation in Christ. Our business ventures grew into multimillion dollar corporations.

Faye and I were active members of a local church and assumed leadership roles in that church body.

In 1983 we were enjoying a wonderful vacation in Acapulco, Mexico, when I sensed the Lord directing me to sell my businesses and enroll in Rhema Bible Training Center in Broken Arrow, Oklahoma.

I obeyed the Lord. Near the end of my training I sensed His direction again, this time to travel to Indonesia with my family before we began serving in the pastorate of what is now known as Victory Christian Fellowship in New Castle, Delaware.

6

The Power of God

Faye and I ministered in Indonesia for six weeks. We traveled with a national evangelist who interpreted for us. But the most profound benefit of our evangelistic effort wasn't so much what happened to the crowds as what happened to the preacher. It transformed my ministry.

While we were in that country, the Spirit of the Lord asked me, "What is your gospel?"

I answered, "My gospel proclaims that Jesus Christ is the Son of God who died for the world." Even though my response was not wrong, I sensed that God wanted to communicate to me something beyond what I was currently perceiving.

"The good news doesn't just *tell about* something," the Spirit of the Lord said to me. "The good news *is* something. The good news is the power of God."

Even though I had gone through Bible school and had been to many churches, I had never thought of it that way before. I knew Romans 1:16: "I am not ashamed of the gospel, because it is the power of God." I had read that passage at least a hundred times. But when the Holy Spirit spoke to me I received a different understanding.

The Lord repeated, "I've given you good news, and that good news is the power of God." The words started rolling over and over in my spirit. Immediately the Holy Spirit led me to various verses in the Scriptures.

First, I read Mark 16:16-18: "Whoever believes and is baptized will be saved, but whoever does not believe will be condemned. And these signs will accompany those who believe: In my name they will drive out demons; they will speak in new tongues; they will pick up snakes with their hands; and when they drink deadly poison, it will not hurt them at all; they will place their hands on sick people, and they will get well."

Before I went to Indonesia, I had been casting out devils and speaking in tongues for several years. So I didn't have a problem there. But when I reached the last two statements—well, I had to work at believing those things were going to happen.

Next, I read Mark 16:19-20: "After the Lord Jesus had spoken to them, he was taken up into heaven and he sat at the right hand of God. Then the disciples went out and preached everywhere, and the Lord worked with them and confirmed his word by the signs that accompanied it." After I finished reading this passage, the Lord said, "I want to give an undeniable witness to this nation that I am alive from the dead."

Well, I knew Indonesia was an Islamic nation and that most of the people did not know my God, even though they have good moral standards and seem to have their lives together.

The main problem with Islam is that the people can't prove their god is alive. So over and over I heard in my spirit, "The good news you have for this nation is the power of God." Then the Lord said, "Declare the power of God! Declare the power of God!"

I thought, Declare the power of God? How do I declare the power of God?

The Spirit replied, "Just demonstrate it."

My attention was drawn to what Paul had said: "My message and my preaching were not with wise and persuasive words, but with a demonstration of the Spirit's power, so that your faith might not rest on men's wisdom, but on God's power" (1 Cor. 2:4-5).

As I meditated on those words I thought, Paul had a different message. He declared Jesus Christ to be the Son of God with power according to the Spirit of holiness.

Paul didn't have a compromising gospel. He never said that sometimes God doesn't perform certain works, as though His power within the believer varied from day to day. Paul knew God's power never changed, for Jesus Christ is "the same yesterday and today and forever" (Heb. 13:8). Paul also never preached that God's power varies depending upon the believer. Since God is no respecter of persons, the same omnipotent power of God is available to all believers.

By the time I finished pondering everything the Holy Spirit had taught me, I was really ready to preach! At my next meeting I preached differently from the way I ever had before.

My interpreter immediately noticed something different. As we progressed to some deeper areas of the ministry, she told me, "I've never said words like these before."

"Don't worry about it," I said. "Just repeat what I say."

35

She responded, "What if He doesn't do it?"

"Well," I answered, "then our God isn't who He says He is."

If you are going to preach this gospel, something has to be settled in your heart. You must believe that everything God says is true and that He will cause those things to be manifest. If He doesn't manifest Himself, then we only have another religion, like Islam. If God doesn't bring results, then this gospel is just a figment of our imagination, trying to convince us there's life after death.

The Jesus I know is the same person Paul mentions in his letter to the Romans, the one "who as to his human nature was a descendant of David, and who through the Spirit of holiness was declared with power to be the Son of God by his resurrection from the dead: Jesus Christ our Lord" (Rom. 1:3-4). The Jesus I'm talking about rose from the dead in resurrection power and walked with the apostles, proclaiming the word with signs following. The apostles preached Jesus Christ, the Son of God, with power.

The Bible says the same Spirit that raised Christ from the dead also dwells in you and me (see Rom. 8:11). The reason God has poured the Holy Spirit upon us can be found in Acts 1:8: "But you will receive power when the Holy Spirit comes on you; and you will be my witnesses in Jerusalem, and in all Judea and Samaria, and to the ends of the earth." This verse says we shall be *witnesses*. That means we will produce evidence that proves to the world that Jesus Christ rose from the dead.

One piece of evidence that I have is the account of my life being transformed by the power of God. I know what happened in me. That is my testimony, my evidence.

I stand today as a testimony to the resurrection power of Jesus Christ. According to Revelation 12:11, that defeats the enemy in my life: "They overcame him by the blood of the

Lamb and by the word of their testimony.'' Jesus Christ is alive! He's present right where you are. He has power and authority to free you from every shackle, burden and weight in your life. He is there to free you from everything that would try to limit you.

In the Acts of the Apostles we read, "With great power the apostles continued to testify to the resurrection of the Lord Jesus, and much grace was upon them all" (Acts 4:33). What was the evidence that Jesus Christ was alive from the dead? Power! The apostles had the Holy Spirit within them as evidence, but the world also needed a visible demonstration of God's power to verify that Jesus was alive.

The apostles' Jesus is the same Son of God who is present right where you are. He hasn't changed one bit! He still heals the sick. We've seen tumors the size of basketballs fall off in people's clothing, as a result of God's power. We've seen deaf people instantly regain their hearing.

God wants you to know that His life within you will triumph over all the works of the enemy. "Therefore God exalted him to the highest place and gave him the name that is above every name" (Phil. 2:9). When Jesus was raised from the dead and exalted, He was given a name to which all things in heaven, in earth, and under the earth would come under subjection. By using the name of Jesus, mankind has received authority.

Today you have the ability to use that mighty name of Jesus at any time. Through Jesus' name you can see blind eyes open, crippled people walk, and demon-possessed people set free. As we have spoken the name of Jesus, we have seen God create limbs and flesh in our hands. By using Jesus' name, we have seen thousands of people born again and thousands of people filled with the Holy Spirit. We have seen these things happen because we have power in the mighty name of Jesus.

There is a testimony inside you that God wants you to let out. He doesn't want your life to be limited any longer by fear of failure or fear of what others might say about you. This new creation life is not a people-pleaser. It's a Father-pleaser. Our new nature wants to say simply, "Father, is that what You want me to do? OK, I'll do it."

We returned from Indonesia with a transformed ministry. Those six weeks marked a turning point in my life.

On August 15, 1984, we launched Victory Christian Fellowship in New Castle, Delaware, with three persons in attendance in addition to my family. Today, some five years later, fifteen hundred people are present each week, with two thousand on our membership rolls.

Along with serving as pastor of Victory Christian Fellowship and founding Victory International Bible Training Centers, I speak and minister in spiritual warfare conferences around the world, relating my own experience of demonic oppression, teaching, and casting out demons. In the remainder of this book I'd like to share with you some of the lessons I've learned about confronting Satan and the work of evil spirits.

7

Works of Darkness

Several years ago in Oklahoma, two other pastors and I went to a mental hospital to minister to a woman. She was in bad shape. She had almost killed a woman, and some family members of the person she injured came and beat her up severely. We went into the locked ward and sat down with her. Her face was contorted from the beating.

The two pastors began by witnessing to her. They led her to accept Jesus as her Savior. She was born again, and a few minutes later she was filled with the Holy Spirit. Hallelujah!

While all this was happening, the Holy Spirit showed me that an evil spirit was attached to the woman's eyes. We hadn't noticed any problems with her eyesight, and she hadn't mentioned any. But there was certainly a demon there. I commanded it to come off her in Jesus' name.

I asked her if she had a Bible. She said no. I took my Bible and said to her, "I want you to read 2 Timothy 1:7. It says, 'For God did not give us a spirit of timidity, but a spirit of power, of love and of self-discipline.' I want you to confess that verse a hundred times."

She read it and reread it. She said, "OK, I will." As she got up, I noticed that the attendant looked at her in a strange way.

That night, the woman's mother came up to us at church and asked, "How's my daughter?"

I said, "Oh, she's doing just great. She got born again and Spirit-filled."

Then I chided the lady a little bit. "Why haven't you ever given her a Bible?"

"Why would I give her a Bible?" she asked.

"So she could read it!" I replied.

She looked puzzled. "But my daughter is blind."

"Your daughter is not blind."

"What do you mean, she's not blind? Didn't you see how the attendants had to take her by the arm wherever she had to go?"

The battered woman's twelve-year-old daughter was standing nearby. I asked her, "Was your mommy blind?"

"Oh, yes," she said. "She had a little path that she used to walk in around the house. She knew exactly where she was going. But when she went to the store, I had to take her by the hand. She hasn't seen in years."

"Well," I said, "she can see now. She's not blind anymore."

I looked at the pastor. "Do you realize what happened? We never prayed for her eyes to be healed. All we did was cast a spirit off her eyes, and she saw.''

The reality was that her problem was not blindness, in terms of a natural condition that needed healing, but an evil spirit that had afflicted her eyes to the point that she could not see. When we cast that demon off her eyes, she saw clearly.

I've seen the same thing happen with deaf people. Now I've prayed for a lot of deaf people who needed re-creation in the inner ear, restoration of a nerve, or something similar. They needed *healing*. But some of the people I've ministered to have had a deaf spirit. They could not hear because a spirit had attached itself to their ears.

I have seen several people who were mute, who couldn't speak. Once an evil spirit was cast from them, they could articulate words.

Evil spirits can cause great affliction and disease in our physical bodies.

I was once in a meeting in Tulsa. I was not ministering, but just sitting there partaking of the teaching. A lady sat next to me. The Spirit of the Lord spoke to me and told me to cast a spirit of cancer off the woman.

This woman didn't look sick. She didn't even look as though she had a problem. But I said, "Well, Lord, I'll do it if You say so."

The Lord said, "Yes, cast that thing off her."

So I tapped her on her shoulder and said, "I don't mean to be rude or anything, but God just spoke to me and told me that you have a spirit of cancer on you. I asked Him further, and He said that you have had several operations for cancer and they never got it all. Is that true?"

She said, "That's exactly right."

"Well, it's not a physical problem we're dealing with; it's an evil spirit. Will you let me take authority over that spirit?"

She was agreeable, so I took authority over it and cast it from her.

The doctors did biopsies after that time of ministry. They checked every one of her lymph nodes and every one of her previously afflicted areas. They found nothing cancerous left anywhere in her body.

My wife and I saw that same lady about two years later. She testified that she has had no further signs of cancer in her body whatsoever.

What was wrong with her wasn't just cancer cells. It was a spirit that was moving from one part of her body to another, afflicting her.

Her body was afflicted by an evil spirit. If we're going to operate effectively as ministers of God's power, we've got to be able to identify where the enemy is operating. If we don't, we're going to be praying for healing when what an afflicted person really needs is deliverance. Or we'll be trying to cast demons off someone when demons aren't the problem at all.

This is where it becomes important for us to understand what evil spirits are and how they operate.

8

The How and Why of Demonic Activity

It's amazing how little people know about evil spirits. The Greek word "demon" comes from a root word *da* that means "to know." A demon is a knowing being, a sphere of knowledge.

Why do people go to palm readers, tea-leaf readers, tarot card interpreters and horoscope experts? To get knowledge. A demon is a knowing being. So what do these mediums produce? Demon knowledge.

Let's examine Deuteronomy 18. It speaks of the occult and of false religions. These are areas in which Satan works.

"When you enter the land the Lord your God is giving

you, do not learn to imitate the detestable ways of the nations there" (Deut. 18:9). All the nations that were in the earth were demon-worshippers. There was only one nation who had the true God. That was Israel. All the other nations had idols.

"Let no one be found among you who sacrifices his son or daughter in the fire, who practices divination or sorcery, interprets omens, engages in witchcraft, or casts spells, or who is a medium or spiritist or who consults the dead. Anyone who does these things is detestable to the Lord, and because of these detestable practices the Lord your God will drive out those nations before you" (Deut. 18:10-12).

Some Christians have accepted practices—like Ouija boards or astrology—that are actually satanically inspired. They say, "Oh, well, they won't hurt me." I want you to know that Satan is out to rob, kill and destroy you.

The Bible tells us where demons come from. "Then another sign appeared in heaven: an enormous red dragon with seven heads and ten horns and seven crowns on his heads. His tail swept a third of the stars out of the sky and flung them to the earth" (Rev. 12:3-4).

Demons were once with God. They are actually fallen angels. When Satan was cast out of heaven, the Bible says his tail drew down a third of the stars of heaven. When the Scripture says stars in this instance, it's dealing with fallen angels.

Anytime you're in a war, you have to understand where the enemy is and what he is doing. What is America investing money in right now? Surveillance, so we can find out what's going on with any potential enemy.

We Christians need surveillance, too. We need to know where and how our enemy is operating. Otherwise we will be caught unawares. The church as a whole has generally been caught unaware of the tactics of the enemy because of lack of knowledge.

My mother had some idea of what was wrong with me—

evil spirits—but she didn't have enough knowledge to set me free. She had to get me to a place where somebody with more knowledge could minister to me effectively and get me set free.

Scripture also teaches us the how and the why of demonic activity. Satan has influence not only in the spiritual realm but also in many other areas. He has influence in our minds. Satan has influence through idols, through the occult, in the political world and in the arrogance of men and women exalted against the Word of God.

As we have seen, demons have influence in the bodies of people.

"While they were going out, a man who was demon-possessed and could not talk was brought to Jesus. And when the demon was driven out, the man who had been dumb spoke" (Matt. 9:32-33).

"Then they brought him a demon-possessed man who was blind and mute, and Jesus healed him, so that he could both talk and see" (Matt. 12:22).

These were not instances of physical healing, but of deliverance. Many physical afflictions are not issues of healing; they are issues of deliverance.

"When they came to the crowd, a man approached Jesus and knelt before him. 'Lord, have mercy on my son,' he said. 'He is an epileptic and is suffering greatly. He often falls into the fire or into the water. I brought him to your disciples, but they could not heal him' " (Matt. 17:14-16).

An evil spirit had this man's son totally under its control. The disciples didn't know what to do with him. I'll tell you, a lot of people didn't know what to do with me, either! I thank God somebody did. People can act very crazy when evil spirits are working in their minds.

"When they came to the other disciples, they saw a large crowd around them and the teachers of the law arguing with them. As soon as all the people saw Jesus, they were overwhelmed with wonder and ran to greet him. 'What are you arguing with them about?' he asked. A man in the crowd answered, 'Teacher, I brought you my son, who is possessed by a spirit that has robbed him of speech''' (Mark 9:14-17).

This passage clarifies what a lunatic spirit is. You might not think that a "dumb spirit" would cause a person to be a lunatic. You might think a dumb spirit would just prevent someone from talking. But it did far more: '''Whenever it seizes him, it throws him to the ground. He foams at the mouth, gnashes his teeth and becomes rigid. I asked your disciples to drive out the spirit, but they could not.'

" 'O unbelieving generation,' Jesus replied, 'how long shall I stay with you? How long shall I put up with you? Bring the boy to me.'

"So they brought him. When the spirit saw Jesus, it immediately threw the boy into a convulsion. He fell to the ground and rolled around, foaming at the mouth.

"Jesus asked the boy's father, 'How long has he been like this?'

" 'From childhood,' he answered. 'It has often thrown him into fire or water to kill him. But if you can do anything, take pity on us and help us.'

" ' "If you can"?' said Jesus. 'Everything is possible for him who believes.'

"Immediately the boy's father exclaimed, 'I do believe; help me overcome my unbelief!'

"When Jesus saw that a crowd was running to the scene, he rebuked the evil spirit. 'You deaf and dumb spirit,' he said, 'I command you, come out of him and never enter him again.'

"The spirit shrieked, convulsed him violently and came out. The boy looked so much like a corpse that many said, 'He's dead' " (Mark 9:18-26).

Jesus later says, "This kind can come out only by prayer" (Mark 9:29).

Sometimes in ministering to those oppressed by demons, we need to spend some extra time before the Lord. Sometimes it's going to take a commitment to fast and pray. However, most of the time we don't have to fast and pray. There have been only a few times when the Holy Spirit has spoken to me to fast and pray to get someone set free. Most of the time we get them set free by simply hearing from the Holy Spirit and speaking in the name of Jesus.

When evil spirits are at work in a person, bizarre and frightening things can happen:

Insanity. In Luke 8:26-36 we find a good example of demons causing insanity. Some of the demoniac's insane behavior is found in Mark 5:2-5.

Cutting or mutilating oneself. Have you ever seen someone cut himself with razor blades, trying to commit suicide? Do you realize that is a demonic activity? Slitting your wrist is nothing new to humanity. Taking sharp stones and trying to cut or kill oneself is common demonic activity in Scripture. (See Mark 5:5.)

Extra physical strength. Faye and I have been in situations where it has taken several people to hold people down until the time they were delivered. I mean some frail little thing with enough strength that it takes five men to hold her down! (See Mark 5:2-4.)

Nakedness. When we were in Indonesia, there was a woman who ran around naked the entire time we were there. She would not wear clothes nor would she live in a house. (See Luke 8:26-39.)

In some Third World countries such people are just walking around in the streets. In those countries Christians are able to minister to them openly. In America we usually have to go into hospitals to minister to them.

9

Demonic Deception

Can a Christian be troubled by demons? There is a raft of teaching that says, "A Christian cannot have a demon." While it may be true that a born-again Christian cannot be *possessed* by a demon, it surely is true that a believer can be *oppressed* by an evil spirit. Some people use the general term "demonized" to indicate that anyone can be troubled to some degree by demons.

Even Simon Peter, only moments after declaring to Jesus by divine inspiration, "You are the Christ, the Son of the living God" (Matt. 16:16), made himself the mouthpiece of the devil. "From that time on Jesus began to explain to his disciples that he must go to Jerusalem and suffer many things at the hands of the elders, chief priests and teachers of the law, and that he must be killed and on the third day be raised to life. Peter took him aside and began to rebuke him. 'Never, Lord!' he said. 'This shall never happen to you!' Jesus turned and said to Peter, 'Out of my sight, Satan! You are a stumbling block to me; you do not have in mind the things of God, but the things of men' " (Matt. 16:21-23).

If Satan can put things into the mind and mouth of Peter, he surely can do so with ordinary believers. Consider this scenario. A husband and wife are involved in a discussion about family finances. Two different viewpoints can be presented, and a rational agreement can be reached. But suppose an evil spirit gets into the act. Suddenly the wife says, "You never think of my needs!" That's a lie, born of that evil spirit, transferred to the woman's mind and spoken through her mouth. Now a giant argument takes place. The evil spirit can leave the scene because his work is done. The fight will rage on, perhaps for days.

Was the woman "demon-possessed"? No. But for a few moments she was open to a subtle suggestion by that evil spirit.

As born-again Christians we don't have Satan's nature, but we can still be influenced by the action of evil spirits. "But how could God and the devil live in the same house?" The simple reality is that while our spirits are born again, our minds aren't. Our spirits are born again, but our bodies aren't. Our minds have to be renewed by the Word of God. Our bodies have to be presented as living sacrifices, acceptable unto the Lord.

Paul teaches the believers at Corinth that they have a warfare in their thoughts. They are to cast down imaginations and pull down strongholds and every high thing that exalts itself against the knowledge of God (see 2 Cor. 10:5).

We don't war after physical beings. The weapons of our warfare are not carnal, that is, sense-oriented. The weapons with which we fight the enemy have nothing to do with what we see, smell, taste, touch or hear. They have to do with "casting down imaginations." And where do imaginations occur? In our minds.

"The Spirit clearly says that in later times some will abandon the faith and follow deceiving spirits and things taught by demons" (1 Tim. 4:1).

There are doctrines of demons out there, leading people to believe things that are simply not true. The key to understanding these demonic doctrines is the word "deceiving."

What is a deceiving spirit? A deceiving or seducing spirit is one that persuades a person to do something disobedient. And a demonic doctrine is any teaching that comes from a spirit other than the Holy Spirit. Any teaching, even if it comes from the most powerful pulpit ministry in the world, must be judged as originating in the Word of God and the Holy Spirit, or it must be set aside.

Demons operate in cults and false religions. Then they do everything they can to get people to believe that there's no harm in them.

I'm talking about things like spiritism, Eastern religions and transcendental meditation. "Oh, but I just do TM to relax!" Maybe, but you're also communicating with demons. Religion, ritualism, formalism, legalism—religious demons are out there promoting doctrinal errors. Have you ever met anybody with a doctrinal obsession? They love their pet doctrine to the distortion of gospel truth.

Demons can operate in the homes of people. "The images of their gods you are to burn in the fire. Do not covet the silver and gold on them, and do not take it for yourselves, or you will be ensnared by it" (Deut. 7:25). Objects of devil worship can ensnare us if we bring them into our homes.

51

Sometimes we go to foreign countries, and people give us something considered to be native art. I check it out and pray over it to find out whether God wants me to have it. Most of the time I say, "No, thank you."

Some people in Panama wanted to give us some little carved dolls. They were cute. But they were also of a type used by spiritists, who would cast a spirit into the doll. Our well-meaning hosts would say, "Would you like to take one of these home with you?" No, thank you! I don't want to bring an abomination into my home and get my family sick, diseased, tormented and confused! "Do not bring a detestable thing into your house or you, like it, will be set apart for destruction" (Deut. 7:26).

Demons play a role in divorce. When Faye and I went through our divorce, it took spiritual warfare to get our marriage back together. I know more people who have not won the conflict of separation and divorce than those who have, because of lack of knowledge of spiritual warfare. If we don't know what's going on, we're going to be destroyed by it. What we don't know can destroy us.

Demons lie to us about prosperity and poverty. Many Christians have a problem with the thought of Christians' prospering. I used to. I believed that poverty was godliness. It's not! Poverty is a curse. It exalts itself against the knowledge of God's Word that breaks the yoke of poverty and releases people to be blessed.

It's often the same with sickness. Some people accept sickness. "Well, God's the one who made me sick." No, the author of sickness is Satan. And God is the one by whose stripes you were healed.

Many people say, "I'm not sure I can believe that." A stronghold is exalting itself, standing up against the knowledge of God, trying to keep us from the experience of healing.

Unforgiveness is a stronghold of the enemy. Have you ever

been tempted to hold unforgiveness against anyone? Scripture says we are to forgive "in order that Satan might not outwit us. For we are not unaware of his schemes" (2 Cor. 2:11). Unforgiveness is an operation of the devil to bind us. It entices us to hold bitterness against another person.

Sexual immorality is one of the greatest strongholds in people's minds. Sexual sins are some of the strongest works of the enemy. In high schools today what's the motto? "Whatever feels good, do it." Why? Because Satan knows that when he can bring a person into sexual immorality, he can bring that person under his control.

Satan is a deceiver. To be deceived means simply to believe something that is not true. Have you ever believed that the sins you have committed in the past and have confessed are currently having a negative effect in your life? That's a false accusation. Satan accuses you that your past, confessed sins are keeping you from having fellowship with God now. If you believe that, you are letting yourself be deceived.

Satan will also try to bring into your mind that you can earn, merit or deserve God's salvation by what you do or don't do—by your works. The letter to the Galatians was written precisely to correct this deception. The Galatians had gone into works, rather than living the life of grace.

Satan is "a liar and the father of lies" (John 8:44). Have you ever said, "I can't," when the Bible says, "I can do everything through him who gives me strength" (Phil. 4:13)? Satan has come to drag you into deception.

"But I am afraid that just as Eve was deceived by the serpent's cunning, your minds may somehow be led astray from your sincere and pure devotion to Christ" (2 Cor. 11:3).

10

The Truth About Satan

The first lesson of warfare is to know your enemy. Our enemy is Satan. Who is Satan? Where did he come from? How does he operate?

Ezekiel describes Satan's beginning:

"You were the model of perfection, full of wisdom and perfect in beauty. You were in Eden, the garden of God; every precious stone adorned you: ruby, topaz and emerald, chrysolite, onyx and jasper, sapphire, turquoise and beryl. Your settings and mountings were made of gold; on the day you were created they were prepared. You were anointed as a guardian cherub, for so I ordained you. You were on the holy mount of God; you walked among the fiery stones. You were blameless in your ways from the day you were created till wickedness was found in you. Through your widespread trade you were filled with violence, and you sinned" (Ezek. 28:12-16).

Satan was the originator of sin. He was found with the nature of sin inside him. "You were blameless in your ways from the day you were created till wickedness was found in you" (Ezek. 28:15). Because of this sin nature, Satan was banished from heaven and was cast to the earth. "So I drove you in disgrace from the mount of God...I threw you to the earth" (Ezek. 28:16,17).

Before man was even created, sin existed. Man was not the originator of sin. Satan was. Satan sinned from the beginning. Man simply hooked up with his sin nature.

People have had various understandings and misunderstandings about Satan, about his position in the earth and his position in heaven. Some people think he's in heaven; some think he's in hell. We need to find out from the Bible what his situation is.

"As for you, you were dead in your transgressions and sins, in which you used to live when you followed the ways of this world and of the *ruler of the kingdom of the air*" (Eph. 2:1-2, italics added). Notice there is one ruler of the kingdom of the air. His name is Satan, "the spirit who is now at work in those who are disobedient. All of us also lived among them at one time, gratifying the cravings of our sinful nature and following its desires and thoughts. Like the rest, we were by nature objects of wrath" (Eph. 2:2-3).

The spirit that controls is called Satan, the god of this world. He has tremendous power to control the human race through the sin nature. We are not just dealing with some little fly. We're dealing with a strong angel, one who used to have dominion over humanity from Adam until Jesus appeared.

Satan, before he was cast out of heaven, was a worshipping angel, who covered the throne of God with praise and glory. He was created by God to give glory and majesty to the King.

"You were anointed as a guardian cherub, for so I ordained you" (Ezek. 28:14). Satan was anointed. He was full of power. He covered the throne of God with praise. He is powerful, not weak. He was an anointed cherub, not a puny weakling with pudgy cheeks and a halo.

But Satan was cast out of heaven because of his rebellion against God.

"Your heart became proud on account of your beauty" (Ezek. 28:17). Satan fell into pride. "You corrupted your wisdom because of your splendor. So I threw you to the earth" (Ezek. 28:17). Heaven is where he was; earth is where he came to dwell.

"I made a fire come out from you, and it consumed you" (Ezek. 28:18). Where did hell come from? Hell was created out of Satan's nature.

"I reduced you to ashes on the ground in the sight of all who were watching. All the nations who knew you are appalled at you; you have come to a horrible end and will be no more" (Ezek. 28:18-19).

Hell was created out of Satan because of his rebellion. Moreover, hell was *not* created for mankind. Jesus said that hell was created for the devil and his angels (see Matt. 25:41).

When we understand that God's grace and goodness are poured out toward mankind and that God's judgment was poured out in wrath against Satan, all of a sudden the gospel becomes clear. God only has one thing He desires to give humanity, and that is salvation. That's good news!

Another description of the enemy's origin is found in the book of Isaiah.

"How you have fallen from heaven, O morning star, son

of the dawn! You have been cast down to the earth, you who once laid low the nations! You said in your heart, 'I will ascend to heaven; I will raise my throne above the stars of God; I will sit enthroned on the mount of assembly, on the utmost heights of the sacred mountain. I will ascend above the tops of the clouds; I will make myself like the Most High' '' (Is. 14:12-14).

The adversary—here called the "morning star"—wanted a higher position. He wanted to rule the angelic host of God. Because of his sin nature, he lost his natural wisdom, his ability to perceive correctly. He lost sight of what he already had. He already had a place in heaven. He already sat above the stars of God. No other angel had such great power.

But when iniquity started to work within him, the Bible says that his wisdom became corrupted. He lost his perspective of what was true and what was real.

Think about it. Why would anybody in the position that the adversary held before his fall ever make statements about seeking greater exaltation? There would be no cause for it. But once the sin nature had arisen in him, he became deceived.

"But you are brought down to the grave, to the depths of the pit. Those who see you stare at you, they ponder your fate: 'Is this the man who made the world a desert, who overthrew its cities and would not let his captives go home?' '' (Is. 14:15-17).

Satan does not open the prison door for anyone. There are people who say, "Well, I can get healed through witchcraft." But no one ever really gets healed through any working of the enemy. They might have an outward manifestation of a change, but ultimately they only have further bondage. I've been in many countries where people had satanic "healings," only to find out they had to be healed by God Himself.

Satan is never the answer to our difficulties. People in

satanic worship cults think they are getting answers. They're not. They're only getting further under the control of the prince of the power of the air who controls them, that spirit that is at work in the children of disobedience.

There are more than two hundred times in Scripture that Satan is mentioned. He's called the prince of the power of the air, the god of this world, the prince of darkness, the prince of devils. He is a king. He's called the anointed cherub, the angel of light, Lucifer, the devil, serpent, adversary, accuser of the brethren, the enemy, the tempter, the wicked one, the thief, the murderer, a roaring lion, a liar, an oppressor, the father of lies. And this isn't all. It's just a sampling.

Let's look for a moment at how Jesus dealt with Satan. He didn't talk about Satan as a figment of the imagination. "Then Jesus was led by the Spirit into the desert to be tempted by the devil. After fasting forty days and forty nights, he was hungry. The tempter came to him and said, 'If you are the Son of God, tell these stones to become bread.' Jesus answered, 'It is written: "Man does not live on bread alone, but on every word that comes from the mouth of God" ' " (Matt. 4:1-4).

Satan is real. He's not a flesh-and-blood person like you and me. You can't punch him and squeeze him so he says, "Ouch!" But he is real nonetheless.

Satan came to Jesus as a person. I'm not talking about flesh and blood. I'm talking about someone who has the characteristics of a person such as a voice, emotion and a will. The Bible says in various places that the devil has a heart, pride, speech, knowledge, power, desire, lusts and other passions.

Satan is as much a person as you are. What makes you a person? Is it just your body? No. It's all the various aspects of your life. Your will, your motivation, your plans, your purposes. Satan has all these. He has everything that makes up a person except a physical body.

Jesus dealt with him as a person in Matthew 4:1-11. He dealt with him directly, just as you would with a person. Satan spoke to Jesus, and Jesus spoke back to him. He didn't say, "I don't believe you exist." Jesus waged war with him as a person. He used the Word of God to defeat him. So must you and I.

"Be self-controlled and alert. Your enemy the devil prowls around like a roaring lion looking for someone to devour. Resist him, standing firm in the faith" (1 Pet. 5:8-9).

11

Power and Authority

When God made us new creations, He not only raised us again from the dead and set us at His own right hand in heavenly places, He also gave us the Holy Spirit in power. Jesus said, "But you will receive power when the Holy Spirit comes on you; and you will be my witnesses in Jerusalem, and in all Judea and Samaria, and to the ends of the earth" (Acts 1:8).

Jesus said we would receive *power*. John wrote, "The one who is in you is greater than the one who is in the world" (1 John 4:4). That's a reference to the Holy Spirit. Jesus quoted Isaiah when He said, "The Spirit of the Lord is on me, because he has anointed me" (see Luke 4:16-21).

When Jesus cast out devils, He cast them out *by the Spirit of God*. It is by the same Holy Spirit that we are able to cast out demons.

Jesus gave us the Spirit. He also gave us something else. "He gave unto [us] power and authority to drive out all demons" (Luke 9:1). Jesus refers to two things. He not only gives us authority, but He also gives us power—power over demons. There is none that exists over whom we don't have power.

The church was ordained by God to have dominion over the enemy and over all the power of the enemy. You and I share in that dominion.

It is one thing to go into the civilized nations, where most people are Christianized already, and go witnessing, knocking on doors. It is another to go in where fetish worshippers are performing their magic and declare Jesus Christ as Lord, then see the "Greater One" rise up and bring the whole tribe to Christ. But I've seen it happen. God has given us power to tread upon serpents, and nothing can stand against us.

We also have authority. How does authority work? Have you ever seen a woman police officer? A megaton truck comes rolling down the road, and the little five-foot, two-inch woman blows her whistle, and that truck driver stands on the brakes and stops. But if someone else stands in the road trying to stop trucks, they just zoom past. What is the difference between that person and the little woman? She has a uniform on that represents *authority*. She represents the whole United States. Every judicial power stands behind her.

It is because of authority that the earth comes under subjection. It is because of authority that the spiritual realm comes under subjection as well. It is not because of might and strength. It is because of the authority that has been given to the Lord Jesus Christ.

God has given us His Spirit. He has given us power and authority. But that's not all He has given us. He has also clothed us with Himself. Romans 13:12 says we are clothed with the armor of light. 2 Corinthians 6:7 says we are clothed with the armor of righteousness. Ephesians 6:11-13 says we are able to put on the whole armor of God.

And even that is not all He has given us. The devil is already running scared, but there's more! God has given us Jesus' name. Philippians 2:9 says His name is above every name.

When we act in His name, we are exercising what is called the power of attorney.

Let me give you an example of the power of attorney. When we were living in Tulsa, we still had a house in Delaware. We had someone else manage the house. We gave them power of attorney so they could manage our affairs for us. They were able to act on our behalf—that is, *in our name.*

Jesus Christ received a name that is above every name, a name to which things in heaven and things on earth and under the earth will bow down. And then He gave power of attorney to man and said, "Go in My name." What does His name represent? It represents *Him.*

We are now far above the devil. We're going to need a microscope to find what he is doing, because of the authority and power that the Son of God has given us.

That's why deliverance is one of the simplest things we can do. We just say, "In the name of Jesus, I command you to leave." We don't have to get all excited because we are in absolute authority. Demons obey our voice. Our problem is, we don't believe it. So we say, "Excuse me, Mr. Devil. Are you sure you're listening to me?" Of course he is!

Jesus says, "And these signs will accompany those who believe: In my name they will drive out demons" (Mark 16:17). And then He said, "Go." Where are we going to go? To wherever serpents and scorpions are—and walk on them. Wherever people are in spiritual blindness and confusion, wherever disease and afflictions of the enemy are, that is where we are to go.

12

New Creation Life

New Testament Christianity is a triumphant life of God's power and dominion in the life of the believer. The church is not to be a weak, sick, beggarly bunch. It is supposed to be a group of believers who know that when Jesus Christ rose from the dead they were born again—just as Jesus Christ was born into resurrection life in absolute triumph and victory.

The problem is that much of the church has been brought under deception by man's wisdom, doctrinal traditions and doctrines of the enemy. Man's wisdom and doctrines of traditional teaching make the Word of God of no effect. So the church, rather than being a triumphant, victorious, over-coming group of believers who are treading upon serpents and scorpions, has been trying to figure out why everything is going wrong.

Jesus rose from the dead to put a new creation man on the face of the earth. God's plan was that the new creation man, Jesus Christ, would be identical twins with every other man and woman who was to be called His brother or sister.

The critical understanding that we must have as believers is that our victory is not based upon ourselves. It is not based upon how strong we are, or how determined we are, or how much we pray. Our victory is based upon Jesus—what He did for us when He rose from the dead. That is where our victory has its foundation.

We are in Christ. When Jesus died, He died with us in Him. The sin nature of the life that we had was in Him. When He died we were in Him, and when He rose from the dead we were in Him.

That is why the Bible says if anyone is in Christ, he or she is a new creature (see 1 Cor. 5:17). What is a new creature like? Like Jesus! There is no difference. We can't separate Jesus and the church. We can't separate the head of the church from the body of the church.

When Jesus Christ became the firstborn from the dead, every new creation man and woman received the same spiritual nature that Jesus had: the same triumph, the same dominion, the same authority, the same provision in life. That's why the church is called "the church of the firstborn" (see Heb. 12:23).

The Bible teaches us that "as he is, so are we in this world" (see 1 John 4:17, KJV). Not "as He is, so are we *trying* to become." A lot of us are trying to become like Him, and we can't. We either are or we aren't. And we are! We are children of God, brothers and sisters of Jesus the firstborn.

Ephesians 2:6 says God has "raised us up with Christ and seated us with him in the heavenly realms in Christ Jesus." When Jesus rose again from the dead, we rose together with Him, so that we are seated with Him in heavenly places—in the same position, in the same authority, in the same dominion that Jesus Himself has.

Angels and principalities are now subject to me because my big brother Jesus and I are together at the right hand of the Father, and everything has been made subject to us. There is not a demon in all creation that is not subject to me or to you. We know that because God's Word says so. We just have to start *acting* as though it were so.

"The weapons we fight with are not the weapons of the world. On the contrary, they have divine power to demolish strongholds. We demolish arguments and every pretension that sets itself up against the knowledge of God" (2 Cor. 10:4-5).

Where does our power for spiritual warfare come from? Ourselves? No! This is why so many people have a hard time with deliverance. They think they have to battle the devil. Well, I have good news. We do. But not on our own.

Paul says in Ephesians 6:10, "Be strong in the Lord and in his mighty power." How are we going to do that? Just believe: I am strong in the Lord and in the power of His might. I live every day that way. I no longer know what it is like to be weak.

Romans 8:37 says that "we are more than conquerors through him who loved us." We are not more than conquerors through our physical, mental or emotional capacities in life. We are more than conquerors through Him.

Jesus Christ is the firstborn from the dead, the firstborn of every new creation. He actually became the forerunner of absolute triumph so that we could live new creation life.

"Both the one who makes men holy and those who are

made holy are of the same family" (Heb. 2:11). We come from the same source. My brother and I come from our father. We and Jesus have that very relationship. That is why "Jesus is not ashamed to call them brothers" (Heb. 2:11).

There are not two different kinds of natures in Christianity. There is only the nature of Jesus Christ—new creation life.

When Jesus rose again from the dead, it was by the Holy Spirit. When you and I are born again, it is also by the Holy Spirit. When we became a new creation, we actually experienced God's power and presence.

When Jesus became the firstborn from the dead, so did we. In a sense we did not get born again in 1970, 1980, 1950 or whenever. We were born again two thousand years ago, when Jesus rose from the dead and brought a new creation man into being. No matter where you were, no matter how it happened, when you said, "I believe in my heart that God raised Jesus from the dead," you realized that *confession* is what brings salvation.

Romans 10:9 says, "If you confess with your mouth, 'Jesus is Lord,' and believe in your heart that God raised him from the dead, you will be saved." What is it that we must believe about the resurrection? That when Jesus rose again from the dead He became the head of a new creation, and that by heart belief we become new creation men and women.

13

Unmasking the Enemy

Before we can minister effectively in deliverance, we've got to be able to see what's going on spiritually. We can't operate on guesswork.

Demonic activity in a person can be detected by our spirits. But our spirits need the Holy Spirit's revelation to be able to see clearly into the spiritual realm.

Paul, in 1 Corinthians 12:8-10, mentions two spiritual gifts that operate in the detection and unveiling of demonic activity. One is the word of knowledge, which reveals what is currently in existence. The other is the discerning of spirits, which enables us to see into the spiritual realm.

There are four spiritual realms: God's angels, demon angels, God's Spirit and our human spirits. The gift of discerning of spirits opens our spiritual eyes to see into those realms. We might see into the spiritual realm with a picture in our mind: while praying with someone, we suddenly see a whole other picture in the spiritual realm.

The gift of discerning of spirits will not only unveil the demonic spirit realm, but it will also unveil the Holy Spirit. It will unveil our spirits. It will unveil God's angels.

Do you want the gift of the discerning of spirits? Ask for it. "Eagerly desire the greater gifts" (1 Cor. 12:31).

Even Christians who do not have a special gift of discerning of spirits can still recognize demons. Scripture says that Satan disguises himself as an angel of light, and so do his ministers. But God helps us see past the disguise.

A demon's presence may be made known to our spirits. Our born-again human spirit is seated with Jesus at the right hand of the Father, far above all principalities, power, might and dominion. It has the capacity for "demon-detection" because of the position of fellowship with God that it has. Thus, because of the light of God's presence that is in our spirits, we can often sense the source of various manifestations.

Have you ever walked into a store, where someone came up behind you, and you felt as if something evil was near you? That is because your spirit is in fellowship with God, and it detects demonic activity.

We are more sensitive to the spiritual realm than we know. The human spirit hears from God. It's in permanent fellowship with the Lord of light, so it detects darkness.

Many times I minister deliverance without the gifts of the Holy Spirit operating in clear words of knowledge, just because my spirit is sensitive to what's going on in the spiritual realm. When people in prayer lines come to me for ministry,

I'm listening for the Lord, and I'm also sensing in my spirit. My spirit is telling me that they are bound. I may not even know anything of what's going on by revelation, but my spirit is letting me know that darkness is present. So I know the avenue in which to minister to them.

Sometimes we can experience what I call "inward knowing." We don't hear a voice or get a mental picture; we just get an inward witness that something evil is present.

When the Holy Ghost tells us something, we should act on it. People have approached me and said, "Gary, I believe there's a demon in my home!"

"What did you do about it?" I asked.

"Well, I came to tell you about it."

"Don't tell *me*," I said. "What am I going to do with it? The Holy Ghost showed it to you; now *you* do something about it. Cast it out in Jesus' name!"

Sometimes we run up against religious spirits, exalting themselves against the knowledge of God's Word. If we're not in communication with the Holy Spirit, we are in danger of being influenced by other voices. We must be aware of danger in the religious area.

This even happened to Paul: "Once when we were going to the place of prayer, we were met by a slave girl who had a spirit by which she predicted the future. She earned a great deal of money for her owners by fortune-telling. This girl followed Paul and the rest of us, shouting, 'These men are servants of the Most High God, who are telling you the way to be saved' " (Acts 16:16-17).

If we stopped here, we would think this girl was really "in the know." We'd think, Get her on TV! She could be a forerunner.

Listen to what she was saying. It appeared to be true. But who was the source of the saying? A demon! "She kept this up for many days. Finally Paul became so troubled that he

71

turned around and said to the spirit, 'In the name of Jesus Christ I command you to come out of her!' At that moment the spirit left her'' (Acts 16:18).

Sometimes we can be in the presence of demonic activity for many days and not have a revelation of what's going on. We just know something doesn't feel right. And then all of a sudden, we know what that thing is! We can deal with it. We don't have to know the name of the demon to cast it out. Notice that Paul did not speak to the demon by name. He just told it to get out. We can do the same.

When dealing with individuals who seem to be troubled by demons, line them up with the Word of God. See if they need to repent of sin. I ask, "Is there anyone whom you have not forgiven?"

"Yes, I'll tell you—I just can't stand so-and-so."

At this point I take them through the Scriptures and explain about demonic door-openers.

"Do you have a lot of strife and envy around the house?"

"Oh, yes, I'm always in strife."

"Where did you get that strife? It says in James 3:15, 'Such "wisdom" does not come down from heaven but is earthly, unspiritual, of the devil.' "

When we know there is demonic activity present, we can line up a person by the Word even if we don't know by revelation what's going on.

The next question is, Will the person submit to God in the area where the Word has shown wrongdoing?

Take, for example, "Husbands, love your wives, just as Christ loved the church" (Eph. 5:25). Let's say a man is bitter against his wife.

"Have you forgiven her?"

"No!"

"Well, you need to forgive her, because if you don't get that sin out of the way, your bondage is going to remain.

You've got to deal with that sin.''

Help the man recognize that he has to ask the Lord to forgive him and then return to loving his wife. Simply have him say, "I choose, in Jesus' name, to love my wife."

Let's look quickly at some of the more common spirits we may face in ministering to people.

Lust. If there has been premarital or extramarital sex, often a spirit attaches itself to the person who was involved. The spirit will carry itself into the marriage and produce an abnormal frustration inside that marriage. The person who has had premarital or extramarital sex needs to be set free.

Division. The same spirits that divided a first marriage will operate in the second marriage. Have you ever noticed anybody going through two or three marriages with exactly the same problems over and over again? Why? It's the same spirit. The marriage partners were never set free.

Rejection. A spirit of rejection will play the same story over and over again in someone's mind. Say the person's mother rejects him. That spirit of rejection hooks onto his mind. He enters his first dating relationship. The girl looks at him funny, and the spirit takes over: "I'm just unlovable. My mother rejected me; you're rejecting me." He gets married. The first time something goes wrong in the marriage, rejection takes over. The same record plays over and over again in his mind. Finally, he is convinced no one loves him. He goes to church and sits alone in a corner. That spirit must be cast out.

Fear of failure. People can have a spirit of fear of failure. They will go so far as to say, "That's it. I just can't go any further, because I failed in the past and I'm going to fail again." The only thing that will turn such a person around is deliverance from that evil spirit.

Of course, there are hundreds of kinds of spirits we might be called upon to remove. These are only a few. But no evil spirit is greater than the name that is above every name, the name of Jesus.

Before continuing, we should note that there are some problems we cannot simply cast out. We cannot cast out sin. We cannot cast out the flesh. We cannot cast out emotions. We cannot cast out the personality of a person. (Sometimes we would like to, but we can't!) Some things are learned behaviors that need to be changed through the knowledge of the Word—these things cannot be cast out.

Many problems are not demonic. Because of ignorance of God's Word, people are living just as the world lives. They committed some particular sin, and they are still committing it. The devil didn't make them do it; James says that people are drawn into sin by their own desire (see James 1:14).

14

Binding and Loosing

The Spirit of God inspired the writers of the Bible to make it clear that our position in Jesus Christ is one of authority, dominion and power. The Holy Spirit enables us, and our human spirit enables us, to identify and locate the operations of the enemy. The only thing that is left is to get rid of him!

Picture one of these devils like a little dog. Like a man walking down the street with a dog nipping at his heels, you say to the pest, "Get away from me. You bother me."

A lot of Christians are like that with the devil. "Devil, just leave me alone today. I want to have a good day."

The devil doesn't respond to that kind of language. He's like that little dog. He might back off a little, but he's right back in another five minutes.

The man walks a little farther with the dog still pestering him. "I said, dog, leave me alone."

The dog backs off a little bit, but soon he goes back after those heels again, nipping and biting.

Finally, the man thinks, I've had it. I'm sick and tired of this dog coming after me and I'm not going to put up with it anymore. And he turns and says, "Now *git!*"

The dog will obey a command like that. So he leaves to find someone else to bite.

Demons understand authority. They understand when you have absolutely, positively, one hundred percent made up your mind about what you're saying. If you have any wavering within you, they will be back.

The Bible speaks of binding and loosing: "...to bind their kings with fetters, and their nobles with shackles of iron" (Ps. 149:8); "...ties up the strong man" (Mark 3:27).

Matthew 16:18 says that the gates of hell shall not prevail against the church. We tend to interpret this in terms of defense. But I want to ask you a question. When have you ever seen a gate attack anybody? The gates of hell were not designed for the church to run from. The church is to break through the gates of hell. The gates of hell do not attack the church; the church attacks the gates of hell.

We have been called by God to be the people on this earth who set at liberty those that are bound, who open the blind eyes, who heal the sick and cast out demons. Our position is absolute dominion, and the proof of our victory is to stop the enemy in Jesus' name at every juncture of life.

Jesus says that He will give us the keys of the kingdom of heaven. Whatever we shall bind on earth shall be bound in heaven. (In the Greek this means "in the heavenlies."

It doesn't mean in heaven where God is.) Whatever we loose on earth shall be loosed in the heavenlies, where the demonic spirit realms operate.

The forces of the enemy have been binding humans—binding their bodies, binding their minds, binding their families, binding their finances, binding their social life, binding their governmental life. These demonic forces have been keeping people from knowing the truth of God's Word by exalting themselves against the knowledge of the truth. You and I have been called by God to release people from these spiritual forces. God has called us as liberators—ones who set others free.

Once we've identified what we're dealing with in the spiritual realm, we then have to do something about it. We can't just say, "Oh, my goodness, I think it's a spirit!" Of course it's a spirit! What else could it be? Now what are we going to *do* with it?

We have to bind it. Binding works by the spoken word. "I bind you in the name of Jesus." By saying, "I bind you," to a spirit in Jesus' name, we restrain its ability to operate. We restrict its behavior.

We can command spirits to be bound in Jesus' name. I highly recommend that any time you're dealing with a spirit, you bind it in the name of Jesus.

Don't allow a spirit to manifest itself. You have authority over whether it manifests itself or not. If the spirit starts carrying on, and the person starts looking a little strange, you command the spirit: "I bind you from manifesting in Jesus' name."

I was ministering in a church in Tulsa. A man said he needed prayer. We went into a tiny side room and started to pray, and he said he was going to get sick. The only person that he could get sick on was me! I said, "No, you're not!" And then I said to the spirit, "In the name of Jesus of

Nazareth, I bind you from manifesting!"

"Oh," the man said, "I feel better!"

"I know you do," I replied.

We don't have to put up with demonic activities. The enemy wants to get a show going if he can. We just don't let the devil put on a show, that's all. After you bind the spirit, if it starts to carry on, bind it from manifesting, in Jesus' name. Then command it out in the name of Jesus.

Paul describes this as "demolish[ing] arguments and every pretension that sets itself up against the knowledge of God" (2 Cor. 10:5). This is not requesting. It is not saying, "Oh, demons, would you mind stepping aside?" They always mind stepping aside.

We have to be violent with demons. The enemy knows that if he is going to say something to me, I'm going to get violent. And I do. I get angry and get it stopped in Jesus' name. I can't afford to have the enemy do to me what he did to me in the past. I've been there once. I'm not going to let him take me back.

The thief comes to rob, kill and destroy. He's not playing games with us. He's out to kill us. He's out to break up our families. He's out to rob our finances. He's out to get us diseased.

We're not playing games. We are engaged in spiritual battles. What we know will cause us to win. What we don't know will cause us to lose. If we know who we are, and we know what to do, then when we do it, we'll win.

Our human spirits have the capacity to stay free from demonic oppression. They are designed by God to live that way. Don't accept defeat. Recognize that Jesus has given you full ability to overcome and win through the power of His mighty name.

Let me conclude this chapter with a few comments about some areas of special importance in spiritual warfare.

Pornography. Keep yourself free from the oppression of the enemy. Ephesians 4:27 says to give no place to the devil. Take, for example, pornography. It's easy to identify this as an area that invites spiritual conflict. Simply say, "Father, in Jesus' name, forgive me. Thank You that I'm forgiven."

Then say, "I break the power of that pornographic spirit and that spirit of adultery in Jesus' name." Now you're free. So what do you do the next time you walk into a store and find out it sells pornography? You don't have to peek over the counter and look at those things. Don't give place to the enemy to influence you. Better yet, don't go to that store or any other that sells pornography!

Unforgiveness. If you know that you've had a challenge with unforgiveness, and someone does something wrong to you, say, "In the name of Jesus, I forgive them. I love them. And I will not give you permission, Satan, to plant a root of bitterness or resentment in me." Get unforgiveness stopped. Right away. Don't give place to the enemy.

Depression. You wake up in the morning, and the enemy says, "It's going to be a lousy day." No! It's never a lousy day. It's always a marvelous Monday, a tremendous Tuesday, a wonderful Wednesday, a terrific Thursday or a fabulous Friday. And don't give place to the enemy's telling you it's going to be a murky Monday, a terrible Tuesday, a weary Wednesday, a turbulent Thursday or a flat Friday.

A lot of people go through their days just existing. Don't just exist—live in triumph! To whom are you going to give place? To whom are you going to give preeminence? Whom are you going to believe? God or the devil?

Use the Word. If you've got an area of challenge that you're overcoming, I encourage you to do this: Write down some pertinent Scripture verses on three-by-five cards. Place these cards on the dashboard of your car or on your bathroom mirror.

Praise the Lord. Saul was relieved of an evil spirit when David played his harp and praised God. Stay in the presence of praise. Why? Because God Himself inhabits the praises of His people.

15

In the Name of Jesus

When we read the story of Satan's original rebellion against God, the thought may occur to us, If Satan was causing God so much trouble, why didn't God just zap him? But the more we understand the Bible, the more we realize why a God of justice would not have done so. Certainly God *could* have dethroned the enemy through an outright display of power. But as we shall see, it is more fitting that God chose to become man to defeat the devil.

When God created the earth, He delegated to man the authority to run the earth. It was man who sold out control of the earth to Satan. So the most fitting way for that authority to be taken back from Satan was for a man to take it back. God wanted it to be a man who took back what man had given away. So God became man in the person of Jesus.

Jesus, as a man, defeated the enemy on the same plane on which the enemy had defeated man. He beat Satan on Satan's home field.

Think about it for a moment. If you were a softball player and wanted to win every game, all you'd have to do is go out with a machine gun and shoot all your opponents. You'd win every game! But would that be just? Of course not. You have to play by the rules in order to win legitimately.

In the same way God, seated on His throne in heaven, has the power to win every game. He could have overthrown Satan by simply zapping him. But He chose instead to come as a man and defeat Satan on the same terms by which Satan had defeated man. God wouldn't think of dethroning the enemy any other way.

The letter to the Hebrews tells us that Jesus suffered everything that every man would suffer. Why? So that He would be in the same sphere, on the same plane as other human beings, being tempted, tried, persecuted, afflicted and abandoned, just as you and I have been. He would live here and die here.

"Since the children have flesh and blood, he too shared in their humanity so that by his death he might destroy him who holds the power of death—that is, the devil—and free those who all their lives were held in slavery by their fear of death. For surely it is not angels he helps, but Abraham's descendants. For this reason he had to be made like his brothers in every way, in order that he might become a merciful and faithful high priest in service to God, and that he might make atonement for the sins of the people. Because he himself suffered when he was tempted, he is able to help those who are being tempted" (Heb. 2:14-18).

The stupefying thing about Jesus' victory over Satan was that He defeated Satan precisely *as* a man.

In Genesis 3:15, God says to the serpent—that is, to Satan—"I will put enmity between you and the woman, and between your offspring and hers; he will crush your head, and you will strike his heel." This was a prophecy that God spoke concerning Jesus Christ, the coming "seed" of the woman, the man who was going to defeat Satan. "The reason the Son of God appeared was to destroy the devil's work" (1 John 3:8).

Satan has tricked us into thinking, Well, Jesus was God, and God could do anything. That's why we're so totally confused about Satan's dethroning. We're not seeing the fullness of victory that Jesus has given to us. If Jesus had defeated Satan purely as God, we would, of course, be grateful. But because He defeated Satan as man, we can actually join in the victory.

When Jesus rose from the dead, He got a name covered with royal power. "And being found in appearance as a man, he humbled himself and became obedient to death—even death on a cross! Therefore God exalted him to the highest place and gave him the name that is above every name, that at the name of Jesus every knee should bow, in heaven and on earth and under the earth, and every tongue confess that Jesus Christ is Lord, to the glory of God the Father" (Phil. 2:8-11).

The devil is defeated by the name of a man! That's why the Bible says to pray in Jesus' name. Our entrance to the Father is on the basis of His humanity and what He did for us as a man. We are given absolute, total dominion and triumph over all the works of the enemy through the power of Jesus' name.

We have a forerunner in heaven—a man with the same nature we have. Jesus was the firstborn from the dead. "He is before all things, and in him all things hold together. And he is the head of the body, the church; he is the beginning and the firstborn from among the dead, so that in everything he might have the supremacy'' (Col. 1:17-18).

What does "firstborn from among the dead" mean? Every other man who had ever died was still dead. Jesus was the first to be "born" from among the dead.

Now there were cases of people coming back from the dead. It was not a common experience, but it had happened before. Remember Lazarus? Jesus said, "Lazarus, come forth!" and he came back to life. Jairus's daughter also came back from the dead. But Jesus did not just "come back from the dead." He was *born* from the dead. There's a difference. Lazarus and Jairus's daughter died again. But not Jesus. He was born from the dead, never to die again.

Jesus was the firstborn from the dead. The resurrection of Jesus Christ was not just God's bringing someone temporarily back from death. It was the bringing forth of a new creation man, one who was going to exist both in heaven and on earth and have total dominion over all the works of the enemy. Jesus was the first. Every believer after Him becomes just like Him.

16

Victory Over the Sin Nature

A major misunderstanding exists among many Christian believers. The misunderstanding is this: that Christians, after they are born again, have two natures. They have a sin nature from which they are never able to get completely free, as well as a nature of God in which they are never quite worthy to walk.

It is critical to see that God has given us absolute victory over the sin nature. If we miss this, our triumph in life becomes only minimal. If we try to battle the enemy on his ground, the sin nature, we are defeated before we begin.

John writes, "He who does what is sinful is of the devil,

because the devil has been sinning from the beginning. The reason the Son of God appeared was to destroy the devil's work'' (1 John 3:8). The phrase "does what is sinful" literally means "continues in the practice of sinning" or "is habitually bound to sinning."

Every person who is not born again is a spiritual child of Satan. Sin is the nature of Satan. He is the first sinner. He sinned from the beginning.

The Son of God was manifested, Scripture tells us, that He might destroy the works of the devil. Well, the first work of the devil is *sin*. When we understand this, we're able to see more clearly what the redemptive work of Jesus Christ has done for us. Then, when we become involved in spiritual warfare, we won't think that we're unworthy, unfit or unable to have dominion and authority over the enemy.

The word *sin*, in the singular, means the *nature of sin*, not *acts of sinning*. The motivation that drives a non-born-again person to sin habitually is the nature of sin. "Sin nature" is the spiritual proclivity inside a non-born-again person. It is not sins, but sin—not wrong actions, but a wrong nature—that separates him from God.

This is why religion that tries to bring a person into fellowship with God through good works is doomed to fail. Good works can never remove the sin nature.

Something creative occurs in a person's life when he is born again. The part of us that is born again is our re-created human spirit. We no longer have two natures. "No one who is born of God will continue to sin, because God's seed remains in him; he cannot go on sinning, because he has been born of God" (1 John 3:9).

Notice, this does *not* say we are not able to commit *sins*. It says we do not commit sin *through the nature of sin*. The sin nature is no longer present within us. When we were born again, the sin nature was broken and removed from us. This was the express purpose for which the Son of God was manifested.

Now every Christian believer can commit *sins*. I'm not suggesting that when you get born again it is impossible for you ever to commit a wrong act. All of us have done wrong things and then asked the Lord to forgive us.

But what causes a believer to sin and what causes an unbeliever to sin are two entirely different things. If we don't understand the difference, we'll find ourselves thinking that the sin nature is causing us to have this monkey on our back from which we can never get free. That's not true.

It all began when Adam and Eve disobeyed God. When they partook of the fruit of the tree of knowledge of good and evil, their natures changed. When they did the thing God said not to do, the very nature of Satan entered into them. That sin nature took over and ruled Adam, his wife and all of their descendants—the entire human race. That's what Paul is talking about when he says, "Sin entered the world through one man" (Rom. 5:12).

And so Paul continues, "In this way death came to all men" (Rom. 5:12). What does this mean? The sin nature passed from one to another through all generations.

Adam brought death to many, but Jesus Christ brings life! "But the gift is not like the trespass. For if the many died by the trespass of the one man, how much more did God's grace and the gift that came by the grace of the one man, Jesus Christ, overflow to the many!" (Rom. 5:15). God's original plan was to create humanity to be in permanent fellowship with Himself. When Satan deceived Eve, Adam fell with her, and they both partook of the satanic nature. God's plan for sending Jesus was to take out of man that spiritual sin nature that had held him captive all of his life. That was the purpose of Jesus Christ's coming to the earth— to remove the sin nature from mankind.

The Bible talks about two "Adams" who have lived on the earth. "So it is written: 'The first man Adam became a living being'; the last Adam, a life-giving spirit" (1 Cor. 15:45). There are two Adams: the first Adam and the last Adam. Who was the first Adam? The one in the garden, the one who ate the apple. Who was the last Adam? Jesus.

"The first man was of the dust of the earth, the second man from heaven. As was the earthly man, so are those who are of the earth; and as is the man from heaven, so also are those who are of heaven. And just as we have borne the likeness of the earthly man, so shall we bear the likeness of the man from heaven" (1 Cor. 15:47-49). Each of us is the offspring of either the first Adam, whose sin nature separates us from fellowship with God, *or* we are born again as spiritual children of God, and the sin nature has been removed from us.

Paul explains how it works. "As for you, you were dead in your transgressions and sins, in which you used to live when you followed the ways of this world and of the ruler of the kingdom of the air, the spirit who is now at work in those who are disobedient. All of us also lived among them at one time, gratifying the cravings of our sinful nature and following its desires and thoughts. Like the rest, we were by nature objects of wrath. But because of his great love for us, God, who is rich in mercy, made us alive with Christ even when we were dead in transgressions—it is by grace you have been saved. And God raised us up with Christ and seated us with him in the heavenly realms in Christ Jesus, in order that in the coming ages he might show the incomparable riches of his grace, expressed in his kindness to us in Christ Jesus. For it is by grace you have been saved, through faith—and this not from yourselves, it is the gift of God—not by works, so that no one can boast. For we are

God's workmanship, created in Christ Jesus to do good works, which God prepared in advance for us to do'' (Eph. 2:1-10).

These lines are written to a church that is not dead anymore. They once were dead. They once were separated, mired in trespasses and sins. But Jesus came to bring to life those who were dead: to remove the sin nature that leads to separation from God.

What redeemed us is not the forgiveness of sins; what redeemed us was the removal of the sin nature. As believers, we still need to be forgiven for the sins we commit. But unbelievers need something more drastic: they need to have the *nature* of sin taken away. And that's just what Jesus came to do.

Jesus Christ died so that the nature of sin would not have control over God's creation. "Yet it was the Lord's will to crush him and cause him to suffer, and though the Lord makes his life a guilt offering..." (Is. 53:10). God made Jesus an offering for sin. The wrath of God was poured out upon mankind, not because of what they did, but because of whose they were. They were children of the devil. The same wrath that was against Satan fell upon mankind and specifically upon Jesus on the cross of Calvary.

Jesus' soul was made sin, not because He wanted to have a sin nature, but because He had to have a sin nature. God had to have a substitute upon whom He could pour all His wrath. Man had to have a substitute to suffer the wrath for him. Jesus Christ, who knew no sin, was made sin for us, that we might be made the righteousness of God in Him.

One of the things that limits us as Christians is that we have not seen the full extent of what Jesus has done for us. He didn't just take out His cosmic eraser and erase our particular acts of sin. No, the Son of God allowed His soul to become the spiritual nature of Satan so He could be a substitute upon which all the wrath of God could be poured out. The Son of God became sin for us so we could be loosed from the nature of sin.

No man killed Jesus. He said, "I lay down my life..." (John 10:17). He willingly took upon Himself the sin nature. Before the foundations of the earth Jesus knew that He would take it upon Himself.

Jesus' death on the cross wasn't a surprise that God sprang on Him in the garden of Gethsemane. Jesus knew He was going to the cross. This was the purpose of His coming to earth, to bear that nature that used to control your life and mine. That was His entire goal. He knew that He would take on Satan's nature on the cross and loose mankind from every shackle with which that sin nature had ever bound him.

"In the same way, count yourselves dead to sin but alive to God in Christ Jesus" (Rom. 6:11). Take a full accounting of the fact that you are not a sinner any longer. Sin has no more dominion, no more control over you. You are a new creation because the nature of sin was removed from you. Reckon fully that you're not a sinner any longer. You needn't walk in guilt and condemnation anymore.

Because of the death of Jesus Christ and the removal of your sin nature, there is nothing to which you are in subjection as far as sin is concerned. The reason why the Son of God died was to remove from humanity that controlling entity called sin nature.

Now you reign triumphantly with Him in righteousness. "Righteousness" means that we stand in the presence of God without inferiority or guilt, just as though sin had never existed, just as though the sin nature was never in us.

That's what you have to see about yourself. When you were born again, the sin nature was removed from you. Now the world, the lust of the flesh, the lust of the eyes and the pride of life have no dominion over you. Not on the basis of how strong *you* are, but on the basis of the death of Jesus Christ. He put you into a position called righteousness. "God made him who had no sin to be sin for us, so that in him we might become the righteousness of God" (2 Cor. 5:21).

17

The Life of Triumph

We do, however, speak a message of wisdom among the mature, but not the wisdom of this age or of the rulers of this age, who are coming to nothing. No, we speak of God's secret wisdom, a wisdom that has been hidden and that God destined for our glory before time began. None of the rulers of this age understood it, for if they had, they would not have crucified the Lord of glory. However, as it is written: 'No eye has seen, no ear has heard, no mind has conceived what God has prepared for those who love him' but God has revealed it to us by his Spirit. The Spirit searches all things, even the deep things of God. For who among men knows the thoughts of a man except the man's spirit within him? In the same way no one knows the thoughts of God except the Spirit of God. We have not received the spirit of the world but the Spirit who is from God, that we may understand what God has freely given us. This is what we speak, not in words taught us by human wisdom but in words taught by the Spirit, expressing spiritual truths in spiritual words'' (1 Cor. 2:6-13).

This passage speaks to us of four sources of wisdom.

The first is our natural reason. This is what tells us, when we're going to drive the car, to get the key. Logic operates in our natural reason. Our minds operate as a reasoning facility all the time.

There is nothing wrong with reason, so long as it doesn't exalt itself against the knowledge of God. For example, reason says, "I can only do what I am able to do in my own strength." The Bible says, "I can do all things through Christ who strengthens me." There is a big difference!

Reason says, "I've only gone through so much schooling, so I can earn only so much money." The Bible says, "My God shall supply all my needs according to His riches in glory in Christ Jesus" (see Phil. 4:19). It says, "If I obey the Word of God, I will be prosperous and successful" (see Josh. 1:7-9).

The next source of wisdom is our flesh. Many Christians are led by the lust of the flesh, the lust of the eyes and the pride of life. They walk about just like an unbeliever.

Have you ever had a lustful thought? That was your flesh speaking. You started getting communication from your body's inordinate affection for something. Or have your eyes suddenly glanced at something, even as you're thinking, I don't want to look at that? It's almost an involuntary action, but it isn't. You can control it. But until you identify the source of what's communicating with your mind, your eyes will be everywhere.

A third source of "wisdom" is the voice of the evil one. Satan can speak to our minds. Strongholds and high things in particular come from the enemy and communicate to our minds. They speak deception, confusion and lust.

James says, "But if you harbor bitter envy and selfish ambition in your hearts, do not boast about it or deny the truth. Such 'wisdom' does not come down from heaven but is earthly, unspiritual, of the devil" (James 3:14,15). There are three qualities of "wisdom" that isn't from above.

First, it is *earthly*. It originates in carnal reasoning. It's quite "reasonable" to get angry at someone because that person did something wrong. But if we stay on that earthly plane, we'll end up in unforgiveness, bitterness and resentment.

Second, it is *unspiritual*, or "sensual." Here the lust of the flesh, the lust of the eyes and the pride of life are speaking to our minds.

Third, it is *of the devil*. The Greek word for "devilish" means "demonic in nature." We can receive "wisdom" directly from demons.

The fourth main source of wisdom is *the Holy Spirit*. We can recognize this wisdom from above because it is "pure; then peace loving, considerate, submissive, full of mercy and good fruit, impartial and sincere" (James 3:17).

Every thought that comes into our minds is easily identifiable and easy to deal with, so long as we know where it is coming from. Let's say you have an antenna on top of your head. The beams from channels 3, 6, 10 and 12 are always bombarding that antenna. Your mind receives the voice of the enemy, the voice of reason, the voice of the flesh and the voice of God through your human spirit all the time. You have within you a spiritual channel selector. Which channel will you choose?

You're driving over the bridge and you get this thought: Drive off the bridge! That surely isn't reason. It's not lust of the flesh, because my flesh surely doesn't want to go into the water. And it's not God, because God doesn't want me to kill myself. So who is it? The enemy.

You wake up one morning. All of a sudden the thought comes: This is a terrible day; everything is going to fall apart; it's hopeless. Is this "wisdom" pure? Is it peace-loving or considerate or full of mercy and good fruit? Of course not. It's not wisdom from above. It's coming from the enemy.

Paul gives us this standard for our thoughts: "Finally, brothers, whatever is true, whatever is noble, whatever is right, whatever is pure, whatever is lovely, whatever is admirable—if anything is excellent or praiseworthy—think about such things" (Phil. 4:8).

As we come to understand these things, we realize that we can identify the sources of wisdom that come to us. Then we have to learn how to shut off the evil channels.

If you find you are receiving from the enemy, simply give the command, "I bind you and command you to stop in Jesus' name."

Perhaps you are hearing from your flesh. Lustful thoughts can be broken instantly. Let's say your eyes are starting to give you a problem. You're looking at something you shouldn't be looking at. Just say, "Eyes, I am dead in Jesus Christ, and you will not be subject to that lust again, in Jesus' name, because it has no power over me."

A lot of us have tried to overcome our flesh with our wills. We can't do it. It's impossible. We're never going to win by trying harder. We win through the death of Jesus Christ. That's where the power is. That's where the victory is over the lust of the flesh, the lust of the eyes and the pride of life.

Reckon yourself indeed dead unto sin. Confess Galatians

2:20: "I have been crucified with Christ and I no longer live, but Christ lives in me. The life I live in the body, I live by faith in the Son of God, who loved me and gave himself for me."

We need not be limited any longer by the words of the enemy, because Jesus Himself has seated us at His own right hand in heavenly places, far above all principality, power and might and dominion and every name that is named, in this world and in that which is to come. We can proclaim, "Satan, if you want to get to me, Colossians 3:3 is how you have to get there. It says I am dead and my life is hid with Christ in God. So for you to get to me, you have to go through God."

Now you're tuned into the channel of God's Word. You're connected to the right source. You've got your channel selector set on the right channel.

Once you've identified the thoughts, then you can curb the tongue. Don't try to stop your tongue until you stop the thoughts, because you'll only get angry with yourself and bite your tongue! You get frustrated. I know people who get mad at themselves because every time they turn around they are saying the wrong thing.

The tongue can be a very destructive entity.

"We all stumble in many ways. If anyone is never at fault in what he says, he is a perfect man, able to keep his whole body in check. When we put bits into the mouths of horses to make them obey us, we can turn the whole animal. Or take ships as an example. Although they are so large and are driven by strong winds, they are steered by a very small rudder wherever the pilot wants to go. Likewise the tongue is a small part of the body, but it makes great boasts. Consider what a great forest is set on fire by a small spark. The tongue also is a fire, a world of evil among the parts of the body. It corrupts the whole person, sets the whole course of his life on fire, and is itself set on fire by hell'' (James 3:2-6).

When we control our thoughts, our tongues can turn the course of people's lives. The same tongue that can bring destruction is the tongue that can bring eternal life to a person. We can declare God's Word, which brings life and understanding.

Don't just "say what you think." Think about what you're thinking before you say anything! Identify the thoughts. You can't afford just to say what you think. You need to identify the source of what you're thinking. If you keep the Word of God in your mind and heart day and night, you will produce in your life the benefit and results of God's Word.

"And we have seen and testify that the Father has sent his Son to be the Savior of the world. If anyone acknowledges that Jesus is the Son of God, God lives in him and he in God" (1 John 4:14-15).

God is love. I want you to know and believe that you are a love child. You are born of love. Your spiritual nature is love. The very nature of God is love, and you are born of God.

Loving people is the easiest thing you'll ever do. Surprised? Don't be. It's a deception of the enemy to think it's hard to love people. "Everyone who believes that Jesus is the Christ is born of God, and everyone who loves the father loves his child as well" (1 John 5:1). If we are born of God, the Bible says that we love God because He first loved us. It also says that everyone who is born of God automatically loves each one that is born of God.

Romans 5:5 says, "God has poured out his love into our hearts by the Holy Spirit." It gushes out of me all the time. There's never a time when I will not turn around and love you. It's an impossibility, because my nature is love. And so is yours. If you want to walk in triumph and victory, believe that the nature of love is inside you, and you can't quit loving. Nothing will be able to stop you from loving because you're born of love.

"For this reason, since the day we heard about you, we have not stopped praying for you and asking God to fill you with the knowledge of his will through all spiritual wisdom and understanding. And we pray this in order that you may live a life worthy of the Lord and may please him in every way: bearing fruit in every good work, growing in the knowledge of God" (Col. 1:9-10).

Take authority. Command the enemy. See yourself dead to sin and alive in Christ. Recognize that you do not have that old sin nature; you have a new creation, righteousness nature. Live in the victory and triumph that Jesus has given you!

Handbook
for
Spiritual Warfare

On the following pages you will find information and Scripture references to help you when you enter spiritual warfare. The topics included are:

Definitions...103
Facts About Demons...105
Demonic Activity...107
Occult Groups and Practices.............................109
Know Your Authority..115
Locating the Enemy...119
Our Weapons Against the Enemy.....................125
Battling the Enemy..129

Definitions

Authority (Matt. 28:18): lawful right in the sense of ability; delegated influences; jurisdiction; power with the legal right to use it.

Bound or bind (Matt. 16:19): any sort of binding; to hold or restrain.

Demon or devils (Luke 11:20): a supernatural spirit (of a bad nature); from the root word "to know," thus, a "knowing being."

Destroy: 1 John 3:8—to render powerless; to loosen; to loose; render free. Rom. 6:6 (the body of sin destroyed)—to render entirely useless; to bring to naught; vanish away; make void. John 10:10—destroy to the full; to mar; die.

High thing (2 Cor. 10:5): an elevated place or thing, spiritual barrier.

Idol (Acts 7:41): an object that attracts demon power. Demons work through idols. They are the spiritual agents in all idolatry. The idol is nothing, but the demon induces idolatry with its worship and sacrifices. An idol draws adoration. It can be anything that assists worship.

Imaginations (2 Cor. 10:5): reasonings.

Know: Rom. 6:6—absolutely know; to know intimately. Rom. 6:9—to know; behold; be aware.

Loose (Matt. 16:19): to unbind, release, to put off, to set free, to discharge from prison.

Power (Acts 1:8): force, miraculous power; ability; strength; mighty (wonderful) work.

Powers (Eph. 6:12): authorities (Greek: *exousiai*).

Principalities (Eph. 6:12): used to describe territories ruled by a prince, ruler, magistrate or leader.

Sin (Rom. 6:7): the spiritual nature in the unbeliever that induces one habitually and continually to commit acts of wrongdoing.

Sins (1 John 1:9): the committing of acts of wrongdoing.

Spiritual wickedness [in high places] (Eph. 6:12): huge numbers of wicked spirits in the spirit world.

Strongholds (2 Cor. 10:4): to fortify through the idea of holding safely; arguments.

Thrones (Col. 1:16): holders of dominion or authority; power or rank of a king; an order of angels.

World rulers (Eph. 6:12): lords of this world, princes of this age.

Facts About Demons

It is important to know about the enemies you are facing.

Demons Name Themselves

Very often evil spirits will name themselves. This is not always the case, nor is it always necessary to know the name of a demon for it to be cast out. We must remember that demons are *liars* and may not be telling the truth about their names, numbers or strength (John 8:44).

What Demons Are Not

Demons are not the spirits of dead people; demons are not the offspring of angels and men.

Where Do Demons Dwell?

They are not in hell. They do have an appointed time of judgment (Matt. 8:29). Demons on earth in Christ's time still inhabit bodies of persons.

What Will Become of Demons?

The devil and his angels will be bound and cast into the bottomless pit (Rev. 20:1-3).

Demons Believe and Tremble

"You believe that there is one God. Good! Even the demons believe that—and shudder" (James 2:19).

Demons Have Willpower

"Then it says, 'I will return to the house I left.' When it arrives, it finds the house unoccupied, swept clean and put in order" (Matt. 12:44).

Demons Have Doctrines

"Things taught by demons" (1 Tim. 4:1).

Demons Are Subject to Christ

"With angels, authorities and powers in submission to him" (1 Pet. 3:22).

Demons Oppose Saints of God

"For I am convinced that...neither angels nor demons...nor any powers...will be able to separate us from the love of God" (Rom. 8:38,39).

"He...not holding to the truth, for there is no truth in him" (John 8:44).

Demonic Activity

Astrology—Deuteronomy 17:3
Blindness and dumbness—Matthew 12:22
Body sores—Job 2:7
Bondage—Romans 8:15
Cities of devil's dominion—Revelation 2:13
Confusion—James 3:16
Convulsions—Luke 4:35
Covetousness, greed—Colossians 3:5; 1 Timothy 6:10
Deaf and dumb—Mark 9:25; Matthew 9:32-34
Divinations—Acts 16:16
Doctrines of demons—1 Timothy 4:1
Envy—James 3:14-16
Evil spirits—Judges 9:23; Luke 7:21
Fear—2 Timothy 1:7
Fear of death—Hebrews 2:14-15
Familiar spirits—Deuteronomy 18:9-12; 1 Samuel 28:7;
  2 Kings 21:6; 1 Chronicles 10:13; 2 Chronicles 33:6
Harm—Matthew 17:15; Luke 8:27-39
Heaviness (depression)—Isaiah 61:3
Infirmity—Luke 13:11-12
Jealousy—Numbers 5:11-31
Kill—John 10:10
Lunatic—Matthew 17:14-21
Lying—1 Kings 22:21-23; Acts 5:3; John 8:44
Nakedness—Luke 8:27
Rebellion—1 Samuel 15:23

Seducing—1 Timothy 4:1
Spirit spoke—Matthew 8:31; Luke 4:33-34; Acts 19:15-16
Strife—James 3:14-16
Tempter—Matthew 4:3
Thief—John 10:10
Unclean spirits—Zechariah 13:2; Matthew 12:43-45;
 Mark 1:23-27; Mark 3:11; Mark 5:2-15; Mark 6:7-13;
 Mark 7:25-30; Luke 4:33-36; Luke 6:18; Luke 8:29;
 Luke 9:42
Whoredoms—Hosea 4:12; Hosea 5:4
World of politics—Daniel 10:13,20

Occult Groups and Practices

All Hallows' Eve: the day witches celebrate above all others, October 31. Considered by witches to be a sacred, deadly and powerful time; a pagan belief.

Amulet: an ornament or gem worn on the body as protection against evil spirits.

Animism: a belief, widely held, especially in Central Africa, parts of Asia, and some Pacific Islands, that souls are quasi-physical and can exist outside the body (in dreams and visions); can be transferred from one body to another; and persist after the death of the body.

Astral projection: the belief that a person can will his soul to leave his body and travel at will to any place in the world or universe. The body is said to be kept alive by a "silver cord" that provides the individual return access. Some fear the danger of the cord being cut or that another spirit would inhabit the unattended body.

Astrology: the art of predicting or determining the influence of the planets and stars on human affairs.

Augury: the practice of divination from omens.

Automatic writing: writing performed without conscious intention and sometimes without awareness, as if of telepathic or spiritual origin.

Bewitch: to fascinate or charm; to affect by witchcraft.

Black mass: a travesty of the Christian mass in devil worship.

Cartomancy: fortune-telling by cards.

Charm: an incantation, especially as a protection against evil or danger; a formula or action supposed to have a supernatural power against evil.

Chiromancy: palmistry, the practice of divining a person's character and future by studying the palm of his hand.

Clairvoyance: a second sight; use of a medium who forecasts distant happenings through visions; ability to know instantly things about people, places or events that were not previously known by the individual through natural means.

Clairvoyant: having second sight; someone who has clairvoyance.

Conjure up: to bring vividly before the imagination as though by magic; to summon up (a spirit) by invocation.

Coven: an assembly of thirteen witches.

Crystal gazer: a person who practices the art of concentrating on a glass or crystal ball with the aim of inducing a psychic state in which divination can be performed; the attempt to predict future events or make difficult judgments, especially without adequate data.

Cult: an unorthodox system of religious worship; a sect; extravagant admiration of or devotion to a person, principle or thing.

Curse: an invocation or prayer for harm or divine punishment to come upon someone.

Demon: an evil spirit; a wicked, destructive creature; an evil attendant power or spirit subservient to Satan.

Divination: a foretelling of the future or the unknown by supernatural means.

Dream incubation: the ritual of sleeping in a sacred place in hope of receiving a divinely inspired dream; recognized by several ancient cultures as a means of guidance and healing.

Enchanter: a magician.

Enchantment: a magic spell or charm; the state of being under a spell.

Esbat: a meeting of witches held for the transacting of business or to accomplish an act of satanic mischief.

Exorcise: to drive out or ward off an evil spirit.

Exorcism: the act or process of driving out evil spirits, commanding them in the name of God to depart, or by using charms, incantations, etc., to free a person or place from the possession of evil spirits.

Extrasensory: outside the senses; involving a source other than the senses; extrasensory perception.

Familiar spirit: a demon who comes at the call of a witch or wizard; a demon who has knowledge of the present or future.

Fetish: an object believed to embody a spirit and exert magical powers.

Fortune-teller: a person who claims to foretell the future and makes money out of the claim.

Graphology: the study of handwriting and the inferring of character or aptitude from it.

Hex: an evil spell; to put an evil spell on; bewitch.

Horoscope: the configuration of the planets, especially at the time of a person's birth, from which astrologers predict his future.

Levitation: the act or process of levitating, especially the rising of a person or thing by means held to be supernatural.

Magic: the art which claims to control and manipulate the secret forces of nature by occult and ritualistic methods. **Black magic:** magic used in the service of evil. **White magic:** use of witchcraft for good. [Note: These are dictionary definitions. Those practicing either black or white magic use occult methods to accomplish *their own purposes*.]

Meditation: to reflect deeply; to spend time in the spiritual exercise of thinking about some religious theme; deep, serious thought; reflection on a religious subject as a spiritual exercise.

Medium: a person credited with special powers for communicating between the living and the dead.

Mystic: a person who believes in mysticism, has mystical experiences or follows a mystical way of life.

Mysticism: a doctrine or belief that direct spiritual apprehension of truth or union with God may be obtained through contemplation or insight in ways inaccessible to the senses or reason.

Necromancy: conjuration of the spirits of the dead for the purposes of magically revealing the future or influencing the course of events.

Observers of time: astrologers.

Occult: beyond the range of normal perception; secret; mysterious; esoteric; dealing with magic and astrology.

Ouija board: a board marked with the alphabet and various signs, fitted with a planchette and used to obtain messages in spiritualist practice.

Palmistry: the practice or profession of foretelling a person's future or reading his character by interpreting the crease lines in the palm and other aspects of the hand.

Poltergeist: a mischievous spirit which manifests its presence by throwing objects about noisily.

Potions: doses of medicine, poison or drugs in liquid form used to bring spiritual blessing or cursing upon an individual.

Psychic phenomena: events which cannot be explained by physical reference and are attributed to spiritual forces.

Psychokinesis: mind over matter; ability to have physical influence over matter (apart from one's own body) through the use of visualization or thought.

Psychometry: divination of facts concerning an object or its owner through contact with or proximity to the object.

Reincarnation: rebirth of a human soul into a new human body.

Rhabdomancy: divination by means of a wand or stick.

Sabbat: main meeting of witches to bring in new members.

Satanic church: refers to any group practicing satanism.

Satanism: worship of Satan, using rites which are a travesty of Christian rites.

Seance: meeting in which spiritualists profess to communicate with the dead.

Soothsaying: predicting the future.

Sorcerer: a person who practices sorcery; a wizard or witch.

Spiritism: the belief that natural objects have indwelling spirits.

Spiritualism: the doctrine that the spirit, surviving after the death of the body, can communicate with persons still living.

Talisman: an object, especially a figure carved or cut at a time considered astrologically favorable, supposed to have magical protective qualities.

Tarot: one of a set of playing cards first used in Italy in the fourteenth century. The figured cards are used in fortune-telling and as trumps in the game played with the entire set.

Transmigration: rebirth of any soul into a different life form.

Voodoo: an Animist religion accompanied by black magic. It was originally African and is still practiced by some cultures in the West Indies.

Witch: a woman practicing sorcery, usually with the aid of or through the medium of an evil spirit.

Wizard: a sorcerer, magician; a person who seems to perform magic.

Know Your Authority

*"And the seventy-two returned with joy and said,
'Lord, even the demons submit to us in your name' "
(Luke 10:17).*

I. New Creation Man—by the Blood

"And they overcame him by the blood of the Lamb
and by the word of their testimony" (Rev. 12:11).

A. *Firstborn of every creature.* "He is the image of the
invisible God, the firstborn over all creation. For by
him all things were created: things in heaven and on
earth, visible and invisible, whether thrones or
powers or rulers or authorities; all things were created
by him and for him. He is before all things, and in
him all things hold together. And he is the head of
the body, the church; he is the beginning and the
firstborn from among the dead, so that in everything
he might have the supremacy" (Col. 1:15-18).

B. *Firstborn among many brothers.* "Those God fore-
knew he also predestined to be conformed to the
likeness of his Son, that he might be the firstborn
among many brothers" (Rom. 8:29).

C. *Brothers to Jesus.* "Both the one who makes men
holy and those who are made holy are of the same
family. So Jesus is not ashamed to call them
brothers" (Heb. 2:11).

D. *Begotten by resurrection.* "Praise be to the God

and Father of our Lord Jesus Christ! In his great mercy he has given us new birth into a living hope through the resurrection of Jesus Christ from the dead'' (1 Pet. 1:3).

E. *A new creation.* "Therefore, if anyone is in Christ, he is a new creation; the old has gone, the new has come" (2 Cor. 5:17).

II. We Are in Him With Power Through Him.

A. *In Him at the right hand of the Father*
  1. Raised together. "And God raised us up with Christ and seated us with him in the heavenly realms" (Eph. 2:6).
  2. Delivered. "He has rescued us from the dominion of darkness and brought us into the kingdom of the Son he loves" (Col. 1:13).
  3. Hidden. "For ye are dead, and your life is hid with Christ in God" (Col. 3:3, KJV).

B. *Power Through God*
  1. Divine power. "The weapons we fight with are not the weapons of the world. On the contrary, they have divine power to demolish strongholds" (2 Cor. 10:4).
  2. Mighty power. "Finally, be strong in the Lord and in his mighty power" (Eph. 6:10).
  3. More than conquerors. "In all these things we are more than conquerors through him that loved us" (Rom. 8:37).

III. We Have the Spirit of God in Power.

A. *Power.* "You will receive power when the Holy Spirit comes on you; and you will be my witnesses in Jerusalem, and in all Judea and Samaria, and to the ends of the earth" (Acts 1:8).

B. *Greater power in you.* "You, dear children, are from God and have overcome them, because the one who

is in you is greater than the one who is in the world"
(1 John 4:4).

C. *God's Spirit.* "The Spirit of the Sovereign Lord is
on me, because the Lord has anointed me to preach
good news to the poor. He has sent me to bind up
the brokenhearted, to proclaim freedom for the captives and release from darkness for the prisoners"
(Is. 61:1).

D. *Yoke destroyed.* "The yoke shall be destroyed
because of the anointing" (Is. 10:27, KJV).

E. *Drive out demons.* "But if I drive out demons by
the Spirit of God, then the kingdom of God has come
upon you" (Matt. 12:28).

IV. Direct Command From Jesus to Have Power and Authority

A. *He gives power and authority.* "When Jesus had
called the Twelve together, he gave them power and
authority to drive out all demons" (Luke 9:1).
"These signs will accompany those who believe:
In my name they will drive out demons; they will
speak with new tongues" (Mark 16:17).

B. *He gives authority over the enemy.* "I have given
you authority...to overcome all the power of the
enemy" (Luke 10:19).

V. We Have Been Given Armor.

A. *Armor of light.* "Let us put aside the deeds of darkness and put on the armor of light" (Rom. 13:12).

B. *Armor of righteousness.* "By the word of truth, by
the power of God, by the armour of righteousness
on the right hand and the left" (2 Cor. 6:7, KJV).

C. *Armor of God.* "Put on the full armor of God so
that you can take your stand against the devil's
schemes. For our struggle is not against flesh and
blood, but against the rulers, against the authorities,

against the powers of this dark world and against the spiritual forces of evil in the heavenly realms. Therefore put on the full armor of God, so that when the day of evil comes, you may be able to stand your ground, and after you have done everything, to stand'' (Eph. 6:11-13).

VI. We Have Been Given the Name of Jesus.

A. *Jesus gives us "power of attorney."*

B. *Jesus' name is above all others.* "Therefore God exalted him to the highest place and gave him a name that is above every name" (Phil. 2:9).

C. *Jesus is alive, and so is His name.* "I am the First and the Last. I am the Living One; I was dead, and behold I am alive for ever and ever" (Rev. 1:18).

D. *Jesus has all authority.* "Jesus came to them and said, 'All authority on heaven and on earth has been given to me' " (Matt. 28:18).

VII. Now Go—in His Name!

"And these signs will accompany those who believe: In my name they will drive out demons; they will speak in new tongues; they will pick up snakes with their hands; and when they drink deadly poison, it will not hurt them at all; they will place their hands on sick people, and they will get well.' After the Lord Jesus had spoken to them, he was taken up into heaven and he sat down at the right hand of God. Then the disciples went out and preached everywhere, and the Lord worked with them and confirmed his word by the signs that accompanied it" (Mark 16:17-20).

All the authority of God is in the name of Jesus in the heavens and the earth, and His name shows forth Him!

Locating the Enemy

I. How to "See" With Your Spirit

A. *Your human spirit (that part of you that is born again as in 2 Cor. 3:6) is in union with God.*

   1. One spirit. "But he who unites himself with the Lord is one with him in spirit" (1 Cor. 6:17).

   2. You are the light. "You are the light of the world" (Matt. 5:14).

B. *Believe you are in the Spirit.*

   1. Controlled by the Spirit. "You, however, are controlled not by the sinful nature but by the Spirit, if the Spirit of God lives in you" (Rom. 8:9).

   2. Don't rehearse doubt by saying that you don't hear God.

   3. Don't be afraid of making a mistake.

C. *Know the operation of your spirit.*

   1. It knows every thought within. "For who among men knows the thoughts of a man, except a man's spirit within him" (1 Cor. 2:11).

   2. It always hears from the Holy Spirit. "No one knows the thoughts of God except the Spirit of God. We have not received the spirit of the world but the Spirit who is from God, that we may understand what God has freely given us" (1 Cor. 2:ll,12).

   3. It spiritually discerns (examines, scrutinizes and

investigates). "The man without the Spirit does not accept the things that come from the Spirit of God, for they are foolishness to him, and he cannot understand them, because they are spiritually discerned. The spiritual man makes judgments about all things, but he himself is not subject to any man's judgment: 'For who has known the mind of the Lord that he may instruct him?' But we have the mind of Christ" (1 Cor. 2:14-16).

4. It knows true wisdom. "The wisdom that comes from heaven is first of all pure; then peace-loving, considerate, submissive, full of mercy and good fruit, impartial and sincere" (James 3:17).

5. It is not double-minded. "But let him ask in faith, nothing wavering. For he that wavereth is like a wave of the sea driven with the wind and tossed. For let not that man think that he shall receive any thing of the Lord. A double minded man is unstable in all his ways" (James 1:6, KJV).

6. It is gentle and quiet. "A gentle and quiet spirit, which is of great worth in God's sight" (1 Pet. 3:4).

7. It receives gifts of the Spirit.
   a. Word of knowledge
   b. Discerning (seeing) of spirits
   c. Gift of faith

8. It keeps himself/herself from the enemy. "We know that whosoever is born of God sinneth not; but he that is begotten of God keepeth himself, and the wicked one toucheth him not" (1 John 5:18, KJV).

D. *Capture the thoughts of God.*
1. Keep thoughts under control. "We demolish arguments and every pretension that sets itself up against the knowledge of God, and we take captive every thought to make it obedient to Christ" (2 Cor. 10:5).
2. Religious taboo ideas contrary to the Word of God must be dropped. "Such regulations indeed have an appearance of wisdom, with their self-imposed worship, their false humility and their harsh treatment of the body, but they lack any value in restraining sensual indulgence" (Col. 2:23).
   a. Formalism
   b. Ceremonialism
   c. Asceticism
3. Don't judge by sight. "And there shall come forth a rod out of the stem of Jesse, and a Branch shall grow out of his roots: and the spirit of the Lord shall rest upon him, the spirit of wisdom and understanding, the spirit of counsel and might, the spirit of knowledge and of the fear of the Lord; and shall make him of quick understanding in the fear of the Lord: and he shall not judge after the sight of his eyes, neither reprove after the hearing of his ears: but with righteousness shall he judge the poor, and reprove with equity for the meek of the earth: and he shall smite the earth with the rod of his mouth, and with the breath of his lips shall he slay the wicked. And righteousness shall be the girdle of his loins, and faithfulness the girdle of his reins" (Is. 11:1-5).

      a. Receive spiritual edification. "He who speaks in a tongue edifies himself" (1 Cor. 14:4). "Build up yourselves in your most holy faith and pray in the Holy Spirit" (Jude 20).

      b. Receive interpretation. "Anyone who speaks in a tongue should pray that he may interpret what he says" (1 Cor. 14:13).

II. How to Identify, Locate and Eradicate

A. *Be aggressive in the Holy Spirit.*

B. *Basic steps for locating the enemy's operation*

  1. Listen to people and use the four sources of wisdom, or knowledge, for identification.

      a. Reason

      b. The flesh

      c. Demon knowledge

      d. God's wisdom

  2. Line up people with the Word.

  3. Examine "door openers."

  4. Has the person repented or is he still involved with the enemy?

  5. Is he submitting to God's will?

  6. Is he actively resisting Satan?

  7. In the natural you may see depression, confusion or fear on the face of a person. This is not always accurate.

  8. What are you hearing in your spirit?

  9. Ask the person what the Lord is showing him in his spirit.

  10. Get the person to pray in tongues with you—before casting out, if possible.

  11. You do not have to know a spirit's name to cast it out—only the area of involvement.

  12. Recognize that it *does* take the Holy Spirit to work with you—"but if I drive out demons

by the Spirit of God, then the kingdom of God has come upon you" (Matt. 12:28).

13. Never assume anything is a spirit: *Know*.

14. Follow Jesus' example in John 5:19: hear, see and do! "I tell you the truth, the Son can do nothing by himself; he can only do what he sees his Father doing, because whatsoever the Father does the Son also does."

Our Weapons Against the Enemy

Name of Jesus

"Through your name we trample our foes" (Ps. 44:5).

"And these signs will accompany those who believe: In my name they will drive out demons" (Mark 16:17).

"In the name of Jesus Christ I command you to come out of her!" (Acts 16:18).

Blood of Jesus

"They overcame him by the blood of the Lamb and by the word of their testimony; they did not love their lives so much as to shrink from death" (Rev. 12:11).

Armor

"Let us put aside the deeds of darkness and put on the armor of light" (Rom. 13:12).

"In truthful speech and in the power of God; with weapons of righteousness in the right hand and in the left" (2 Cor. 6:7).

"The full armor of God" (see Eph. 6:11-13).

God's Ability, Authority and Power in Us

"When Jesus had called the Twelve together, he gave them power and authority to drive out all demons" (Luke 9:1).

"Even the demons submit to us in your name" (Luke 10:17).

"I have given you authority to trample on snakes and scorpions, and to overcome all the power of the enemy; nothing will harm you" (Luke 10:19).

"But if I drive out demons by the Spirit of God, then the kingdom of God has come upon you" (Matt. 12:28).

"But you will receive power when the Holy Spirit comes on you" (Acts 1:8).

"The weapons we fight with are not the weapons of this world. On the contrary, they have divine power to demolish strongholds" (2 Cor. 10:4).

"For he has rescued us from the dominion of darkness and brought us into the kingdom of the Son he loves" (Col. 1:13).

"And having disarmed the powers and authorities, he made a public spectacle of them, triumphing over them by the cross" (Col. 2:15).

"Be strong in the Lord and in *his mighty power*" (Eph. 6:10, italics added).

"Which he exerted in Christ when he raised him from the dead and seated him at his right hand in the heavenly realms, far above all rule and authority, power and dominion, and every title that can be given, not only in the present age but also in the one to come" (Eph. 1:20-21).

"Who has gone into heaven and is at God's right hand—with angels, authorities and powers in submission to him" (1 Pet. 3:22).

"That by his death he might destroy him who holds the power of death—that is, the devil" (Heb. 2:14).

"God raised us up with Christ and seated us with him in the heavenly realms in Christ Jesus" (Eph. 2:6).

"The one who is in you is greater than the one who is in the world" (1 John 4:4).

"And the yoke shall be destroyed because of the anointing" (Is. 10:27, KJV).

"The Spirit of the Sovereign Lord is on me, because the Lord has anointed me to preach good news to the poor. He has sent me to bind up the brokenhearted, to proclaim freedom for the captives and release for the prisoners" (Is. 61:1).

Battling the Enemy

"Put on the full armor of God so that you can take your stand against the devil's schemes. For our struggle is not against flesh and blood, but against the rulers, against the authorities, against the powers of this dark world and against the spiritual forces of evil in the heavenly realms"
(Eph. 6:11-13).

Follow these guidelines when encountering evil spirits:

I. Be Sensitive to the Spirit of God.

    A. *Revealed by God.* "Jesus said, 'Blessed are you, Simon son of Jonah, for this was not revealed to you by man, but by my Father in heaven. And I tell you that you are Peter, and on this rock I will build my church, and the gates of Hades will not overcome it. I will give you the keys of the kingdom of heaven; whatever you bind on earth will be bound in heaven, and whatever you loose on earth will be loosed in heaven' " (Matt. 16:17-19).

    B. *Satan will try to trick you and make you ask, "What's in it for me?"*

II. Be Firm and Constant in God's Promises.

    A. *"Be self-controlled and alert.* Your enemy the devil prowls around like a roaring lion looking for someone to devour. Resist him, standing firm in the faith, because you know that your brothers throughout the world are undergoing the same kind of sufferings'' (1 Pet. 5:8-10).

B. *"We do not want you to become lazy, but to imitate those who through faith and patience inherit what has been promised"* (Heb. 6:12).

III. Be Bold and Authoritative in Confrontation.

"...and to make plain to everyone the administration of this mystery, which for ages past was kept hidden in God, who created all things. His intent was that now, through the church, the manifold wisdom of God should be made known to the rulers and authorities in the heavenly realms, according to his eternal purpose which he accomplished in Christ Jesus our Lord. In him and through faith in him we may approach God with freedom and confidence. I ask you, therefore, not to be discouraged because of my sufferings for you, which are your glory'' (Eph. 3:9-13).

IV. Bind the Spirit in Jesus' Name.

A. *Bind to restrict the demon's activity so the casting out is far less violent.*

B. *Bind the spirit from manifesting and speaking.*

C. *Bind the strong man and spoil his goods.* "In fact, no one can enter a strong man's house and carry off his possessions unless he first ties up the strong man. Then he can rob his house" (Mark 3:27).

D. *Bind their kings.* "...To bind their kings with fetters, their nobles with shackles of iron, to carry out this sentence written against them. This is the glory of all his saints. Praise the Lord" (Ps. 149:8,9).

E. *Bind on earth.* "Jesus replied, 'Blessed are you, Simon son of Jonah, for this was not revealed to you by man, but by my Father in heaven. And I tell you that you are Peter, and on this rock I will build my church, and the gates of Hades will not overcome it' " (Matt. 16:17-19).

"I tell you the truth, whatever you bind on earth will be bound in heaven, and whatever you loose on earth will be loosed in heaven. Again, I tell you that if two of you on earth agree about anything you ask for, it will be done for you by my Father in heaven. For where two or three come together in my name, there am I with them" (Matt. 18:18-20).

V. Command the Spirit Out in Jesus' Name.
  A. *Paul said, "In the name of Jesus Christ I command you to come out of her!" (Acts 16:18).*
  B. *Exercise authority, not knowledge or arguments.* Demons hear authority, not volume.
  C. *Cast out devils.* "And these signs will accompany those who believe: In my name they will drive out demons; they will speak in new tongues" (Mark 16:17).
  D. *Cast down imaginations.* "We demolish arguments and every pretension that sets itself up against the knowledge of God, and we take captive every thought to make it obedient to Christ" (2 Cor. 10:5).

VI. Resist Actively and Aggressively.
"Submit yourselves, then, to God. Resist the devil, and he will flee from you" (James 4:7).

VII. Wrestle, Not as an Equal Opposite

"For our struggle is not against flesh and blood, but against the rulers, against the authorities, against the powers of this dark world and against the spiritual forces of evil in the heavenly realms" (Eph. 6:12).

VIII. Pull Down Strongholds

"The weapons we fight with are not weapons of the world. On the contrary, they have divine power to demolish strongholds" (2 Cor. 10:4, KJV).

IX. Stand Firm and Immovable Against the Enemy.

A. *Ability to stand.* "Put on the full armor of God so that you can take your stand against the devil's schemes" (Eph. 6:11).

B. *Having done all, stand.* "Therefore put on the full armor of God, so that when the day of evil comes, you may be able to stand your ground, and after you have done everything, to stand" (Eph. 6:13).

X. Keep Yourself.

"We know that anyone born of God does not continue to sin; the one who was born of God keeps him safe, and the evil one cannot harm him" (1 John 5:18).

XI. Give No Place.

Once you become spiritually alert, Satan cannot just enter your life, so don't give him any opportunity. "Do not give the devil a foothold" (Eph. 4:27).

XII. Use the Word.

A. *It is written!* "Jesus answered, 'It is written: "Man does not live on bread alone, but on every word that comes from the mouth of God." '...Jesus answered him, 'It is also written: "Do not put the Lord your God to the test.' "...Jesus said to him, 'Away from me, Satan! For it is written: "Worship the Lord your God, and serve him only" ' " (Matt. 4:4,7,10).

B. *The wisdom of God preached to the devil and spirits.* "His intent was that now, through the church, the manifold wisdom of God should be made known to the rulers and authorities in the heavenly realms, according to his eternal purpose which he accomplished in Christ Jesus our Lord. In him and through faith in him we may approach God with freedom and confidence" (Eph. 3:10-12).

Preach to the devil about the power of the blood. "They overcame him by the blood of the Lamb and by the word of their testimony; they did not love their lives so much as to shrink from death" (Rev. 12:11).

XIV. Praise the Lord.

A. *Put on the garment of praise.* "...And to provide for those who grieve in Zion—to bestow on them a crown of beauty instead of ashes, the oil of gladness instead of mourning, and a garment of praise instead of a spirit of despair. They will be called oaks of righteousness, a planting of the Lord for the display of his splendor" (Is. 61:3).

B. *God inhabits praise.* "Yet you are enthroned as the Holy One; you are the praise of Israel" (Ps. 22:3, KJV).

C. *Saul was delivered when David sang.* (See 1 Sam. 16:14-23.)

D. *Jehoshaphat sang out praises; God sent ambushments.* "After consulting the people, Jehoshaphat appointed men to sing to the Lord and to praise him for the splendor of his holiness as they went out at the head of the army, saying, 'Give thanks to the Lord, for his love endures forever.' As they began to sing and praise, the Lord set ambushes against the men of Ammon and Moab and Mount Seir who were invading Judah, and they were defeated'' (2 Chron. 20:21,22).

XV. Prayer and Fasting

A. *"This kind goeth not out but by prayer and fasting" (Matt. 17:21, KJV).*

B. *God's chosen fast.* "Is not this the kind of fasting I have chosen: to loose the chains of injustice and untie the cords of the yoke, to set the oppressed free and break every yoke?'' (Is. 58:6, KJV).

    1. To loose the chains of injustice

    2. To untie the cords of the yoke

    3. To let the oppressed go free

    4. To break every yoke

XVI. Breaking Evil Words

A. *The Word is sharper than any two-edged sword.* "For the word of God is living and active. Sharper than any double-edge sword, it penetrates even to dividing soul and spirit, joints and marrow; it judges the thoughts and attitudes of the heart'' (Heb. 4:12).

B. *We break other swords.* (See Ps. 64.)

C. *Condemn judgmental words.* " 'No weapon formed against you will prevail, and you will refute every tongue that accuses you. This is the heritage of the servants of the Lord, and this is their vindication from me,' declares the Lord'' (Is. 54:17, KJV).

XVII. Don't Ever Quit in Spiritual Warfare!

Remember, it is not over until you have won!

"We have heard with our ears, O God; our fathers have told us what you did in their days, in days long ago. With your hand you drove out the nations and planted our fathers; you crushed the peoples and made our fathers flourish. It was not by their sword that they won the land, nor did their arm bring them victory; it was your right hand, your arm, and the light of your face, for you loved them. You are my King and my God, who decrees victories for Jacob. Through you we push back our enemies; through your name we trample our foes. I do not trust in my bow, my sword does not bring me victory; but you give us victory over our enemies, you put our adversaries to shame. In God we make our boast all day long, and we will praise your name forever'' (Ps. 44:1-8).

As a reader of this book you may request a *free* cassette tape by Gary V. Whetstone on spiritual warfare. Please write to:

Victory International Bible Training Center
P.O. Box 10050
Wilmington, DE 19850-0050